TECHNICAL ANALYSIS
DEMYSTIFIED

Other Titles in the Demystified Series

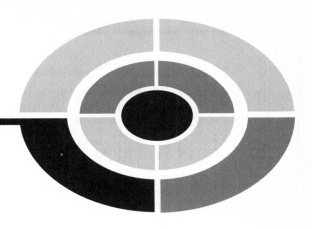

Technical Analysis
Demystified

CONSTANCE BROWN

New York   Chicago   San Francisco   Lisbon
London   Madrid   Mexico City   Milan   New Delhi
San Juan   Seoul   Singapore   Sydney   Toronto

Copyright ©2008 by Constance Brown. All rights reserved. Printed in the United States of America. Except as permitted under the United States Copyright Act of 1976, no part of this publication may be reproduced or distributed in any form or by any means, or stored in a data base or retrieval system, without the prior written permission of the publisher.

1 2 3 4 5 6 7 8 9 0 FGR/FGR 0 9 8 7

ISBN-13: 978-0-07-145808-5
MHID   0-07-145808-5

This publication is designed to provide accurate and authoritative information in regard to the subject matter covered. It is sold with the understanding that neither the author nor the publisher is engaged in rendering legal, accounting, or other professional service. If legal advice or other expert assistance is required, the services of a competent professional person should be sought.

—From a Declaration of Principles jointly adopted
by a Committee of the American Bar
Association and a Committee of Publishers

McGraw-Hill books are available at special quantity discounts to use as premiums and sales promotions, or for use in corporate training programs. For more information, please write to the Director of Special Sales, Professional Publishing, McGraw-Hill, Two Penn Plaza, New York, NY 10121-2298. Or contact your local bookstore.

Library of Congress Cataloging-in-Publication Data

Brown, Constance M.
  Technical analysis demystified / by Constance Brown.
      p. cm.
ISBN-13: 978-0-07-145808-5 (pbk. : alk. paper)
ISBN-10:   0-07-145808-5

  1. Investment analysis. 2. Stock price forecasting. I. Title.
HG4529.B7633 2008
332.63'2042–dc22   2007023005

This book is printed on acid-free paper.

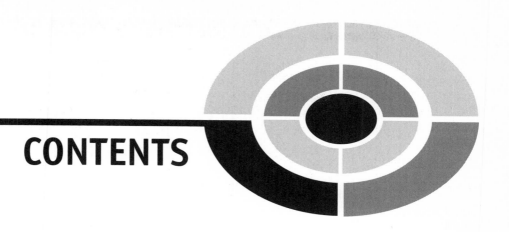

CONTENTS

Preface

The phone was ringing. Small ice granules mixed with rain tapped on my window as the phone announced the expected call from London. The caller's e-mails had shown me that he was in trouble, but I did not know why.

The caller was eager to talk about gold. It was clear that his stress was tied to the open positions he held in several gold stocks. Gold recently had been screaming upward. At first glance it was hard to see why the caller would be in such distress at a time when his position was moving in a favorable direction. However, before answering his questions, I had a few questions of my own. I wanted to know what his *planned* exit strategy had been when he had bought the stock. In reply, the caller stated in a low voice, "I don't have one."

Then I wondered how long he had been trading and what methods he used to make trading decisions. He rattled off a line that brought to mind what the Scarecrow repeated after receiving his brains from the Wizard in the 1939 film *The Wizard of Oz*. The Scarecrow recited the following mangled form of the Pythagorean theorem: "The sum of the square roots of *any* two sides of an isosceles triangle is equal to the square root of the remaining side." The caller had the Scarecrow's tone of confidence when he spouted several technical inconsistencies. The caller had the same problem, as he was fairly close but definitely incorrect.

I asked the caller, "What percentage of your trading capital was allocated to gold?"

"Why, all of my trading capital is in gold. Is that a problem?"

That is not just a problem. It is a catastrophic error that the caller would have realized if he had known the math behind that approach. My next question would identify whether he had been trading short-term market swings or his focus was on the longer-horizon trend only.

It took little time to discover that the caller had bought stock in gold mining companies in 2003, his first experience in any market, and then had no idea how to get out. He never scaled back at times of risk before corrections, he never added to his original order size, and it was clear that he didn't have a clue about what to do with this gold bull he had grabbed by the horns. If he let go, he would be gored! It was now three years later, and the stress was unbearable. He made the following statement: "I have been an active trader the last three years." Because he had entered a single buy order nearly three years earlier, he had knighted himself with the title of *trader*. He had no idea how to trade the swings and no concept that the gold market was about to form a significant top before experiencing a major correction. When I asked, "How would you feel about a $100 drop in gold?" he gasped and asked, "Could that happen?" After thinking for a moment, he added, "Well, then I would exit my positions with a profit!" I told him, "Not only could this happen, it is about to happen, and the start of the decline is less than a week away."

I then asked, "What would you do if gold then made a full recovery and made a new high?" He answered, "You cannot possibly know that in advance, can you?"

This person was not a trader. He had no idea when to bank some or all of his profits, no idea when to expect a large or small correction, and no concept of when to take partial profits so that he could increase his position after a countertrend decline into a target area. He did not know how to determine whether the larger trend was complete. He had no tools or methods in place to control his financial risk and, worse, he had no concept of the risks he faced.

The rain started coming down harder, making it difficult to hear the caller. The timing was perfect because I needed to take a deep breath. The hardest people to teach or guide have a false sense of confidence despite their limited experience. It was little wonder the caller was under stress. He had no controls in place, and the train he was on was a runaway. Gold was in a fast rise, and he had no tools to answer the basic questions he needed to ask. Forget the answers; he did not know the questions to ask himself. His internal negative pole was working, but he was not listening to it. Because he wanted to talk to me, I could see that he knew he needed to bank some profits. However, greed would not let him believe what he already knew. I decided to be more direct than tactful since he was about to hit a brick wall.

Preface

Many people have this misunderstanding. They open and close a position and suddenly believe that that makes them a trader. However, you are *not* a trader until you can answer these questions:

1. What price level is my target for this stock or market *before* I get in? When that target is realized, I can tell whether the stock or market will respect or exceed my target. I know what to do with my current position in either situation because I have planned ahead of time what action I will take.

2. What price level should the stock or market *not* pass through? I know how to exit a position and reestablish the same position *in a manner that decreases my risk and improves my return.*

3. What methods can I use to increase my probability of having the correct opinion about the market?

4. Can I list the strengths and weaknesses of the methods I use to give myself permission to open or close a market position?

5. What does *element-of-ruin* mean?

6. What does the word *leverage* mean, and do I know how to calculate the correct position size for the financial risk to my bank account?

"Can you answer these questions?" I asked. The caller gasped and said, "I don't think I could answer any of those questions, but I can tell you what the last four earnings reports for Newmont Mining contained."

Great, I thought. The London caller's *Titanic* is sailing full steam to New York and will never see the iceberg in its path. This phone call took place in February 2006. By September 2006 Newmont Mining had fallen from $60 to $40. It turned out that we had spoken right at the top. I wonder if the caller took any action before the decline hit.

Fundamentals cannot answer any questions about timing, assess the *real-time risk* for a current market position, or warn you when a large bump in the road is fast approaching. You can buy and sell any stock or market with the click of a button. In a fraction of a second you can see the confirmation of your actions on the computer screen. You smile as your first efforts succeed, and you extrapolate from your daily gain by multiplying the number of days in a year by the number of years you have ahead. Success! You are a gifted trader. Right? Wrong! Not until you can answer the questions above and a host of others.

I made this statement to the caller: "Fundamentals cannot answer the majority of the questions surrounding trading." He responded in a disbelieving tone: "Why

not?" I explained that fundamentals do not provide the risk management tools that give a trader longevity. Without technical analysis to improve market timing in volatile markets, the markets may devour you. In fact, the market *will* devour you if you have no concept of the element of ruin. The caller meekly asked, "Element-of-ruin; what is that?"

I gave the caller a harsh wake-up call that night in February.

Could you have answered the questions I asked the gold trader? Perhaps some, but not all if you are just beginning. All traders start with limited knowledge and no experience. What makes the difference between someone who survives the early years and someone who blows up? The answer is not knowledge but risk management. Having control of your risk buys you time to develop knowledge of the markets.

Before we continue this discussion, let me share an experience I had with a different novice trader. This is an example of what happens when someone with little experience believes he or she knows enough to join extremely advanced traders in a seminar with specific prerequisites.

The novice trader strongly believed in her current skills. She knew she had more to learn, *but everything she currently knew surely was being applied correctly*, she felt. She primarily traded oil stocks and had been in the market during a period when oil basically went in one direction: up. She had a very strong view about what she needed to learn to go forward. Usually, this kind of confidence comes from objective experience. If you are blindly confident and a beginner in any field, that confidence may be a mixture of ego and arrogance. This is a deadly combination since it puts one's inner balance out of alignment. Being a good trader requires continued work on the inner poles of personal balance.

Tiger Woods was interviewed and said something very pertinent to trading. The essence of his message was that golf is played on a course six inches long. He then raised his hands and pointed to the sides of his head. Trading is very similar because traders need a mix of confidence in their tools, humility toward their markets, and knowledge about their personal strengths and weaknesses.

Our paths first crossed when this trader contacted me to join my advanced trading seminar. To her disappointment, I explained that she would not qualify for the course because she would hold the others back. She was missing many of the basics and had some very odd views about what she needed to learn. For example, she stated that risk management was of no interest to her. If she survived much longer in the market, her need to gain a better understanding of ways to control risk would become clear. Her current perspective revealed a lack of experience.

A few months passed, and she was very persistent about attending the seminar. I was working on the outline of this book at that time, and it seemed like an opportunity to help her and test the level of my material. I always respect some-one who makes a commitment to learn because that is what it takes to become a good trader.

We decided to meet with the understanding that she would be the "test pilot" of a new book for beginners. However, after her visit I nearly abandoned the book project entirely. What happened?

This woman could not see that a $5 drop in a $90 oil stock was not the same thing as the three-year total meltdown that unfolded in the NASDAQ! She was angry when I asked her about stocks she had never traded. It was clear that her anger was directed at herself because she had studied many books and believed that she was knowledge-able about the markets. Perhaps she was comparing herself with her family and friends, but she had never been given a scale to measure her progress and found the reality of how much she didn't know frightening.

What I found surprising was her belief that she did not need to learn anything that did not provide a direct buy or sell signal. Not only could she not see huge dif-ferences between charts, she was angry that I did not agree that a $5 drop in a high-priced oil stock was a devastating correction. She had no sense of proportion or scale when looking at a chart and judged a chart on the basis of *what she personally had experienced*. She had lost money in the oil stock's correction, and that was what made the decline a devastating move.

Although listening to one's inner voice can be valuable, it is necessary to control one's emotions. There are tools that allow a trader to predetermine his or her worst-case scenario before taking action. At one point I asked her to identify an unknown market from a monthly chart of the Japanese Nikkei crash. I was not expecting her to recognize the Nikkei, but she did need to suggest any market that was like it in character. She could not identify it or suggest it was the NASDAQ or any other market that had experienced a historical crash.

I would not have cared if she had named the Nikkei, the NASDAQ, the tulip bulb mania, or the real estate crash of 1897 when some buyers awoke to find they had purchased land under the Hudson River in New York. A market crash is a crash in any language, and the mass public mania that unfolds looks the same each time, with a parabolic rise that leads to a full retracement.

She was angry that I had "tricked" her, feeling that it had been unfair to show her a market chart of Japan's index. Japan had nothing to do with oil, she stated. I explained that all of Japan's oil has to be brought into the country from overseas. The price of oil would be affected by growth in China as well. An awareness of Asian markets was important to traders in North America. She then stated, "Oil would never crash." Even the Internet stocks were old stories about the "dot-gones."

I knew the markets would chew her up with that attitude and felt the need to ask another question when we discussed a price target for one of her oil stocks.

I asked, "How much of your trading capital do you commit when the market enters your target price zone for this one stock or trading idea?" I was expecting an answer such as "Maybe 10 percent," "I am not sure," or "I don't know." It is usually a good idea to answer a question like that with a simple "I am not sure." But she shocked me with a sudden confident answer: "Why, *all* of it, of course!" I gasped and said, "No! You cannot risk more than 10 percent of your capital on a single idea and survive. I would go as low as 3 percent total when you are just beginning, and that includes all your correlated positions."

"But that is outrageously small!" she disagreed in an angry tone. I described something called the element-of-ruin, a mathematical fact that if you over-bet, you will lose your entire bank account *regardless of how brilliant your stock timing and picks may be.*

It is a term best known by professional blackjack players. It is the mathematical probability that a player or team of players will lose their bankroll when the shoe, or deck of cards, swings against them. In a trader's case, a bankroll is a trading account. It may surprise you that traders are bound by the same rules as card players.

Professional blackjack is not gambling; it is a set of fixed rules and measurable risk exposures expressed mathematically, usually expressed in percentage form. In 1981, Ken Uston wrote in his book *Million Dollar Blackjack* that his teams always used a 5 percent element-of-ruin; that meant that his team's bets were calibrated to yield a 19-out-of-20 chance of doubling a bank and a 1-out-of-20 chance of going broke. Any activity that involves a negative string of events or positive string of outcomes has to be analyzed mathematically so that you can survive. If you bet your entire bankroll, it does not matter how brilliant you are: You will be blown out of the markets.

A look of fear crossed her face. The math was sound. I only hope I raised enough fear to buy her a little time to experience the markets longer than her first year.

Although the stories of these two novice traders are different, involving one who was focused on gold stocks and one who traded oil stocks, both traders lacked any plan or skills to protect themselves. When traders begin, they lack knowledge and experience, and that leads quickly to a lack of money to trade. That means a trader will be not be able to gain any experience. For this reason it is more important for a beginner to have risk management in place before developing chart knowledge and market experience. Why? *Because risk management buys traders time to learn.* Did you know that the Chicago Mercantile Exchange reports that 96 percent of all

Preface

S&P futures traders lose money? The 4 percent who are winners are taking it from the losers. Stocks are more forgiving, but the majority does not win.

My goal is to improve your odds for success. Do not be afraid, just realistic, because success in trading requires work and preparation. With an open mind to learn and grow, you can enjoy years of working on a global market puzzle that is ever changing and evolving. That makes it endlessly fascinating, and your patience in being willing to prepare well will be rewarded, making it time well spent. Are you ready?

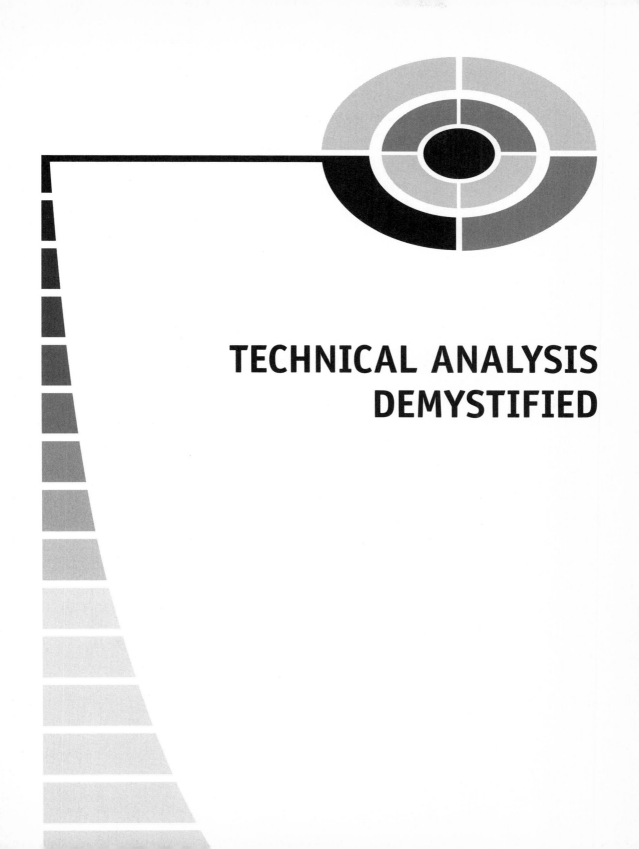

TECHNICAL ANALYSIS
DEMYSTIFIED

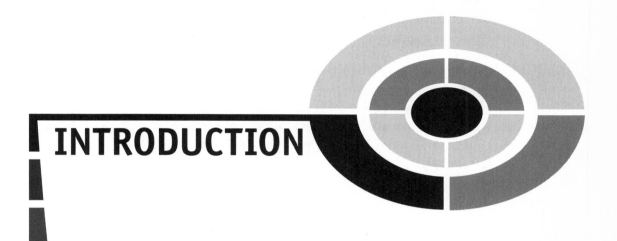

INTRODUCTION

In the financial markets, now more than ever, timing is everything. When should you get into a market, and, perhaps more important, when should you get out? Every trader, whether in futures, currency, bonds, or stocks, would like to know what the market is going to do before it actually does it.

Many economists say that this is impossible, that price-affecting events are basically random and unpredictable, and that there is no way to "beat the market." Nonetheless, a growing number of Wall Street veterans know from experience that there *is* a way to identify trends, anticipate when those trends will reverse themselves, and predict with reasonable accuracy how big the corrections will be. That method is called technical analysis.

Technical analysis is the term used in the financial world for a fairly diverse set of methods unified by one basic conviction: The behavior of markets is not random but occurs in accordance with patterns that repeat themselves over time. Some of those patterns are easy to perceive, but mostly they are subtle and can be revealed only by mathematical modeling. Technical analysts rely on graphs or charts of historical price data to reveal the patterns; that is why they are nicknamed *chartists*. The competing approach to markets is known as *fundamental analysis*, and so-called fundamentalists believe that the most important things to know are business statistics such as corporate cash flow and price-earnings ratios. If you don't know the facts on the ground about the entities you are trading, asks the fundamentalist, how can you make investment decisions about those entities?

A chartist would reply that all the relevant information is embodied in the price whether you realize that or not. Besides, in today's global, fast-paced trading environment, it is not possible to master all the data about companies and commodities, much of which may not be available in English. Finally, there is one essential force in the market that fundamental analysis cannot account for: human psychology. Market participants, no matter how they like to think of themselves, are not always rational actors. A brief glance at financial history shows that greed, fear, and crowd following have been major factors in booms and busts. Since technical analysts believe that all forces affecting the market are by definition reflected in price levels, those forces must include the particularly elusive force known as *investor sentiment*.

You may be surprised to learn that technical analysis has a venerable history. The first known use of it was in eighteenth-century Japan, where rice was traded by members of the samurai warrior class at the Ojima market in the city of Osaka. By around 1710 that pursuit had evolved from simple rice trading to the buying and selling of rice contracts, thus creating the world's first futures market. A particularly astute trader, Munehisa Homma, noticed the effect of traders' emotions on rice prices and in 1755 attempted to quantify it in a book called *The Fountain of Gold: The Three-Monkey Record of Money*. He broke markets down into bullish and bearish varieties, observed that each type of market contains the seeds of the other, and represented price changes with a system of bar graphs called *candlesticks* after their distinctive appearance.

Homma's achievement was unknown outside Japan until relatively recently, so the credit for pioneering modern technical analysis goes to Charles Dow, the financial journalist and founder of Dow Jones. In a series of editorials in the *Wall Street Journal* at the end of the nineteenth century, Dow identified three different kinds of trends, arguing that an apparent trend is meaningful only when it is accompanied by high trading volume and that it should be assumed that a trend will continue until there is definite evidence that it has ended. Finding that point remains the key task of the chartist, and Dow's successors have devised various methods of doing so, along with increasingly elaborate conceptual models. The search for inherent patterns continued in the early twentieth century as analysts saw market movements reflecting geometric principles respecting Universal Laws. In the 1920s, basing his analysis on mass psychology, Ralph Nelson Elliott propounded the Elliott Wave Principle, which traces the rhythmic movements inherent in mass psychology. Much more recently, George Lane invented stochastic analysis, a method that focuses on the momentum of price to identify overbought and oversold excesses.

Introduction

Nowadays you don't have to be a mathematician to perform technical analysis. Personal computers and an ever-growing variety of software options make it possible for the ordinary intelligent trader to benefit from the theoretical brilliance of innovators such as Lane and Elliott. Data vendors make a huge amount of price information available over the Internet. This book will help you use those resources to create your own charts for the investments you are interested in, whether stock markets, money markets, or real estate. You will learn how to use indicators to read future price movement that is "buried" in the historical price data.

It is important to bear in mind that technical analysis is both a science and an art. There are no quick and easy answers, no single algorithm that always tells you what to do. A successful trader must not rely on only one method and needs to develop sensitivity to the markets' periodic vibrations. Eventually, you will narrow down the plethora of oscillators and methods of analysis and decide on a core group of market indicators that work for you. When you reach that point, you will be able to "time" the market and increase your profits while effectively managing risk.

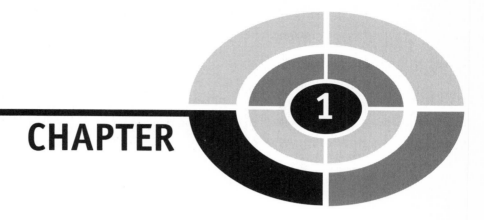

CHAPTER 1

How Do Past Prices Indicate Future Prices?

A First Look at Reading Charts

History does repeat itself. Professor W. C. Mitchell made the following statement in 1950 during a lecture at Harvard University: "Business history repeats itself, but always with a difference... because it is the outgrowth of the preceding series of events."

Someone in the past assuredly foresaw the current business climate. The first book published in North America that discussed future market movement was *Benner's Prophecies of Future Ups and Downs in Prices, Third Edition* by Samuel

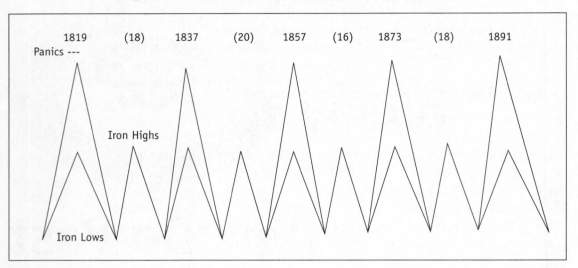
Figure 1.1 *Benner's Prophecies,* Samuel Benner, 1875, (page 105)

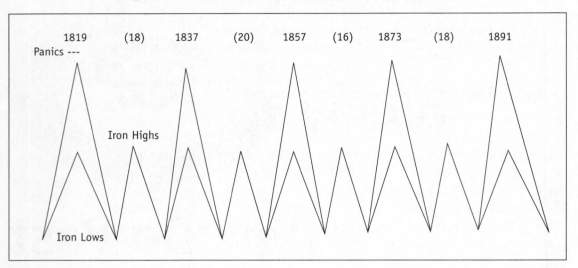

Benner (Cincinnati: Robert Clarke & Co., 1884). The first edition, published in 1875, gave the observations and forecasts of an Ohio farmer whose predictions were brilliant. Benner's book mapped market sentiment highs and lows for the iron, pig, and corn markets and gave forecasts for panic cycles. The same chart was extended to include the modern years when Robert Prechter copied Brenner's work from the 1875 publication of the book. Prechter's chart of panic cycles was widely acclaimed, though few knew the chart's original source was published in 1875. Figure 1.1 shows the chart as it was redrawn and printed in *Benner's Prophecies.*

The Ohio farmer was not the first to document business cycle history. That honor falls to the Swiss historian and economist J. C. L. de Sismondi (1773–1842), whose treatise brought attention to the effects of commercial crises and economic factors on politics and cultural development.

Dr. Hyde Clarke, an English statistician who wrote in *Herapath's Railway Magazine,* developed this early analysis of cycles further in 1847. Clarke's paper *Physical Economy—A Preliminary Inquiry into the Physical Laws Governing the Periods of Famines and Panics,* described the panic conditions of 1847 as they related to panics in 1837, 1827, 1817, 1806, and 1796. He also divided the 54-year period between the famine at the time of the French Revolution and the then-current famine in England into five intervals of 10 or 11 years. The European famines of 1793, 1804, 1815, 1826, 1837, and 1847 identify an 11-year cycle that still affects business conditions.

Samuel Benner wrote the following in his 1875 book:

If we could have yearly average prices of corn for the whole country since 1825, we would find that they would show the same regularity in ups and downs that they do after 1862. The Finance Report of 1863 in giving prices for the New York markets (which are a long ways from corn producing states) shows that prices were very high in 1825, 1826, in 1836, 1837, in 1847 and 1858. The statistics of the Department of Agriculture show that the average price was very high in 1864; in fact higher than ever before in this country; and again the price is at the top figures in 1869 (for corn). The average price for 1875 will be high, and it is the next high priced year after 1869. These high priced years correspond with the price of hogs. These years are the highest priced years since 1830, making eleven-year cycles up to 1858, afterwards in short cycles of six and five years. The next high priced year for corn, which is in the future, will be the year 1880, eleven years from 1869, and five years from 1875.

Benner went on to discuss the cycle of 11-year lows in stock prices. His forecast for 1880 was fulfilled, and his little book became famous. A hundred years later Robert Prechter repeated the cycle.

A theory advanced in December 1867 by John Mills before the Statistical Society of Manchester, England, stated, "Business cycles are essentially credit cycles which are determined by the rates, confidence, and the mental mood of businessmen." This was the first documented reference to sentiment as a key factor in the economic climate.

Technical analysts often are involved with behavioral sciences. Trading is a study of mass psychology and human nature common to most individuals. We will conclude this book with a closer study of how trading is not just the act of buying and selling. But to begin our journey in discussing the basic concepts it is important to recognize that market conditions tend to be repeated in rhythmical patterns. It is as if the lessons learned by one generation fail to be passed on to the next. Human nature ventures out on its own accord and therefore stumbles into the same holes, though the hole may be shaped and positioned in a different place and time. Technical analysts like to see historical charts that go as far back as possible. In 1931 Dr. Warren M. Persons, a professor of economics at Harvard University, wrote the following in *Forecasting Business Cycles:*

The world of affairs in which we live is not a mechanistic world; it is a bewildering world of multiplicities, complexities, interactions, repercussions and the vagaries of human wants, fears and hopes. It is a world in which, at times, facts and logic become subordinated to human emotions. At such times individuals, who by themselves are rational, join with other rational individuals to form an unreasoning mob.

Persons in effect was providing further support to the mental mood theory introduced by Mills in 1867. More important, he was describing the way mass public sentiment becomes a force within a complex environment. Have economists forgotten their roots of studying human nature in favor of looking at modern statistical extrapolations based on questionable corporate summaries? Today, technical analysts track mass public sentiment through chart work. We also look for industry group discrepancies. Only charts showed that the corporate collapse of Enron was possible because the chart was a misfit to its group and had no technical reason for holding its sustained climb. We didn't know why it was out of step, we just knew something was horribly wrong. Technical analysis gave advance warning Enron was in trouble when the fundamental picture could offer none to the public.

Modern technical analysts have an additional edge over economists trying to keep up with our Global village in numerous languages: We can visually track all the global markets rapidly to find inconsistencies and imbalances. No individual can track all the fundamental reports and statistics released around the world. For example, how well can a fundamentalist track the relevant factors in China in a timely way? As the world becomes smaller and its boundaries become less rigid, the work of chartists bridges language, geography, and complex trade routes in a timely manner.

Economists focus more on extrapolation these days, reasoning that if it was so in the last 4 to 5 years, it must be so for the next year as well. However, business is a cycle of changing sentiment, as has been stated in the work of some of the best economic historians. Economists are mere participants in cycles of overexuberance that change to cycles of fear, protection, and extreme caution. When business conditions are expansive, it is easy to overextend because credit is easy to obtain. Then, when business starts contracting, few lending institutions want to take on risk and history shows that smaller businessmen and businesswomen lead a nation out of trouble.

Technical analysis makes it easier to spot these repeating cycles of extremes since it is rare to find oneself in a balanced, steady portion of the pendulum swing.

Measuring Market Sentiment

Technical charting can be used to measure market sentiment in several ways. Consider how price data can form patterns on charts. Imagine a bear market that has been declining for many months. Eventually the smart money begins to recognize an opportunity, and that group of foxes begins to buy and hoard stocks before the majority of market participants do. The majority still believes that the old trend remains in force, and the chance to sell the market crushes the new rally. If the underlying strength of the market is gaining more buyers than sellers, the market will fail to make a new market price low.

The fact that a new price low was attempted and failed is a flag to experienced traders and investors that a genuine change is in the wind. Analysts read in their charts that the selling pressure in the market has weakened as fewer sell orders are reaching the exchanges. The ratio of buyers to sellers is tracked through the actual volume data collected by the exchanges. Now more people jump onboard with the early foxes who guessed that a change was near. As the buying increases, there comes a time when the majority ends up on the same side of the market, desperate to buy.

Here is the way the desperation manifests: If you have been bearish and your losses hurt too much when the dollar loss becomes extreme, you have to cover your positions by buying. If you were one of the early buyers in the new trend, you are trying to buy more. If you were on the sidelines, left out of the party, you suddenly are under pressure to jump in. Thus, at one point in a rally everyone is trying to do the same thing.

Later in the buying cycle the laggards who were left out entirely or got out too soon will pray for a decline so that they can join the party. At about this time the early buyers want to bank their profits, and so they cause a corrective pullback. The laggards jump in and run the market to another new advance. That is when the party ends because too few participants remain to buy into the market at the new levels. Thus, the cycle repeats because it has become overextended. A setback now is required before the cycle can renew itself.

This cycle of human sentiment creates geometric patterns that can be measured. One school of technical analysis and chart reading requires a solid foundation in basic geometry. Those who work with charts all the time see balance, proportion, and ratios without using tools to measure the basics. One's eye becomes so trained to see geometric rhythms and balances in price action that it is easy to overlook how many areas of geometry one uses. You do not need the underlying equations that mathematicians use, just the conscious awareness that geometry with proportions and balance has to be applied to the many price swings within a chart.

Basic Geometry Review

The graph in Figure 1.2 illustrates a market price point that is really a position within a rectangular space. To identify this position, one uses the old mapmakers' coordinate system, which is known as *Cartesian coordinates*. Call the current price of a stock point P. It is known that it occurs on a certain day, at a certain level, and at a certain distance from zero. Therefore, the current market price really has an address on 3 perpendicular spatial axes that generally are named x, y, and z.

Markets are charted with time shown along the x-axis, with the oldest data appearing on the left. The price values rise along the y-axis. The z-axis along the diagonal line in the chart is really the same fixed distance as x is from y, like the depth within a cube.

Figure 1.2 A Market Price Point

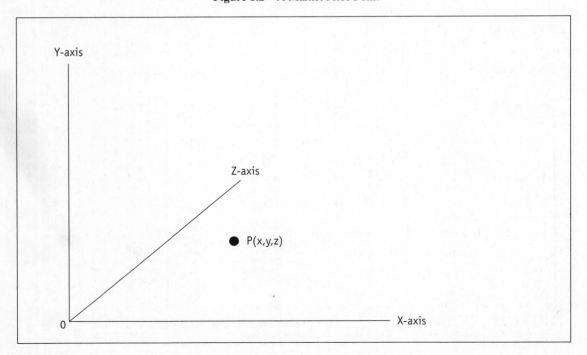

A market price at point P is describing *motion*. Consider a market rally that lasts for 8 weeks. The market starts at a price low and moves to a new price over time. How long did it take? How fast was the rally in comparison to the prior move? These are questions associated with motion.

If Microsoft (MSFT) starts the 8-week period at $23 and ends at $28, we can study one example of chart geometry using the slope of a line. (The slope is found by dividing $y_2 - y_1$ by $x_2 - x_1$.) If MSFT was trading at $23 on Monday, that date would be the value for x_1. If the stock traded at $28 ten trading days later, that date would be x_2. The values for y are the price levels at which y_2 equals $28 and y_1 equals $23. The slope indicates *the rate of the rise or fall of the price action*.

Consider a price low for MSFT of $23 at the start of a move, after which the price high forms at $28. This price high is followed by 3 days of downward prices, and so the $28 high is looking like a distinctive high now. Draw a line from the start to the end. The line forms a straight path, and so it will cut through the price data in the middle. This line will indicate the health of MSFT and the potential risks associated with trading the stock.

Figure 1.3 shows a gold stock called Newmont Mining (NEM). The chart indicates that it had a sharp decline that was followed by a rally that retraced the earlier downtrend. The rally ends sharply at point C. The two price bars at C create a market directional signal we will study in Chapter 5. This chart can be used to connect the starting and ending price levels. These moves are called *market swings*. Connect the price high at A and the price low at B and then connect the same price low at B to the more recent price high at C.

The rally looks very steep, and so does the decline. The question is as follows: Can you determine whether the rally was as steep as the decline? If you think they are the same, you need to work on your geometric "eye."

Figure 1.4 provides several opportunities to answer that question. One way to begin making the comparison is to draw a straight line upward from the price low. Can you tell whether the angles a and c are different? If you move to the middle, a horizontal line is drawn from the decline to the vertical line in the center. A horizontal line then is drawn from the center to the rising swing. Can you see that line d is longer than line b? Could you have seen the difference if the horizontal line had been drawn at a lower level? Still having trouble? You can draw a horizontal line higher up in the chart and increase the comparison ratios even more. Look at line bd and line ef. It should be clear that line ef is longer than line bd. Do you see the two right-angle triangles you created?

If a straight line had been drawn from the price high at A to the *x*-axis and another straight line had been drawn from the price high at C to the *x*-axis, you

Figure 1.3   Monthly Chart for Newmont Mining

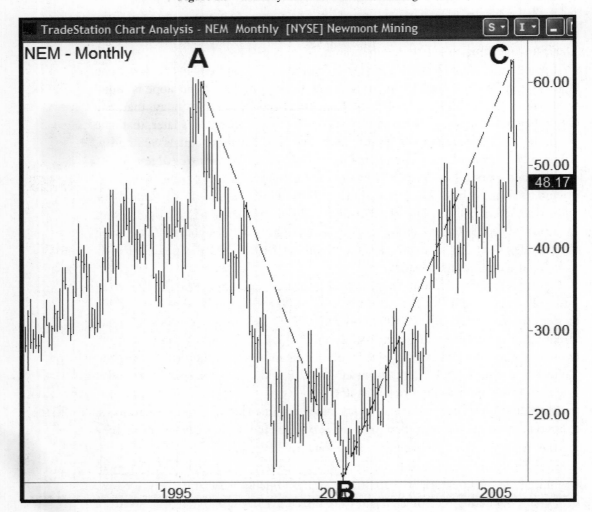

could have used the separation of the points along the x-axis to answer the question. Because the price highs are similar, the time the market took to go from price high A to the low at B was less than 5 years. The time required for NEM to return to the high exceeded 5 years. Therefore, the rising swing is not as steep or *fast* as the decline it is being compared with in this chart. We are in fact comparing the slope of the two dashed lines.

How did time and speed suddenly enter the discussion? Math wizards say that the distance traveled divided by the time is called the speed. Technicians have taken

Figure 1.4   Comparison of the Decline and Rally in Newmont Stock

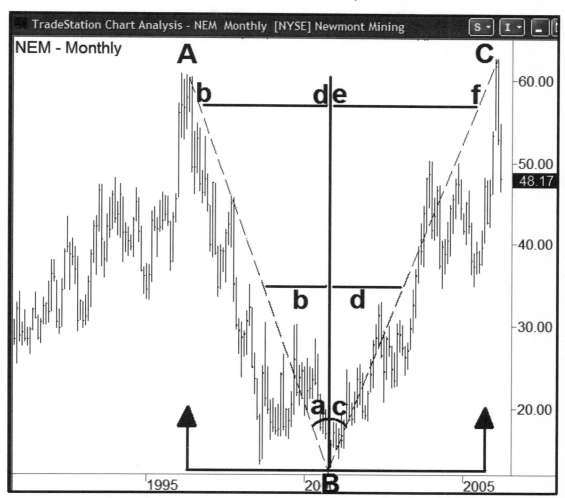

from elementary physics the concepts of time and speed. In fact, technicians often use speed lines to help them make judgments about the market.

   First we applied basic trigonometric functions without all the math mess, as I refer to it. We wondered if the stock price action had formed an isosceles triangle between the decline and the follow-up rally. This is a triangle with at least two equal sides and hence two equal angles. We saw that the market decline was faster than the returning rally after comparing the angles, computing the slope of a line, and referring to time.

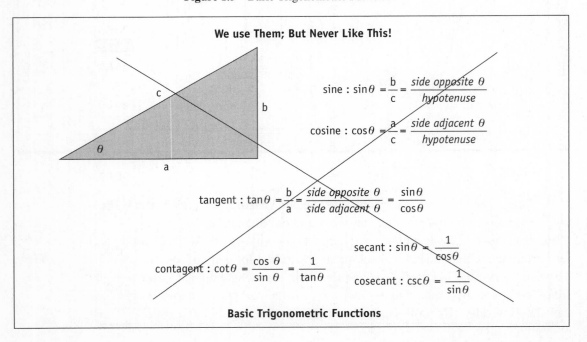
There are three kinds of triangles: obtuse, acute, and right. An obtuse triangle has one angle greater than 90 degrees. Only one of the angles can exceed 90 degrees or it no longer would be a triangle with three connected sides. An acute triangle is one with every angle measuring less than 90 degrees. A right triangle has one 90-degree angle. There are two right triangles in Figure 1.4. Within the triangle the longer side opposite the right angle is called the hypotenuse. This is the line you drew on the price decline from A to B or drew from B to C in the case of the rally. It was the vertical line from the low that connected the backs of the two right triangles.

You were asked to consider the angle that formed from the price low to the lines drawn from the price highs. However, you never had to work with the trigonometric functions behind this application because you only had to make a visual comparison to determine whether one angle was different from another. It was not necessary to get involved with the mathematical notations behind the applications (see Figure 1.5).

The most advanced market geometry employed today is called *Gann analysis*. It uses all four disciplines of higher education from ancient times: the quadrivium. The four disciplines are geometry, music, astronomy, and number theory. Technical analysis will tap college electives you once studied or interests you currently have in

Figure 1.5   Basic Trigonometric Functions

We use Them; But Never Like This!

$$\text{sine} : \sin\theta = \frac{b}{c} = \frac{\text{side opposite } \theta}{\text{hypotenuse}}$$

$$\text{cosine} : \cos\theta = \frac{a}{c} = \frac{\text{side adjacent } \theta}{\text{hypotenuse}}$$

$$\text{tangent} : \tan\theta = \frac{b}{a} = \frac{\text{side opposite } \theta}{\text{side adjacent } \theta} = \frac{\sin\theta}{\cos\theta}$$

$$\text{secant} : \sin\theta = \frac{1}{\cos\theta}$$

$$\text{contagent} : \cot\theta = \frac{\cos\theta}{\sin\theta} = \frac{1}{\tan\theta}$$

$$\text{cosecant} : \csc\theta = \frac{1}{\sin\theta}$$

Basic Trigonometric Functions

ways you never imagined would apply to finance. Geometry is important here because markets move in rhythmic proportions and ratios. Markets are masses of people reacting to fear, greed, and cyclical rhythms. Every 20 years a new generation has to learn for itself what the last generation learned the hard way. The oscillating human emotions of greed and hope or panic and fear create cyclical patterns of rising and falling price swings. This is a simple example, but the deeper one goes into watching and learning how mass groups of traders become and react as a collective body. (The study of cycles can be a specialization that stands on its own.)

Consider the internal price swings in Newmont Mining stock shown in Figure 1.6. The full decline is subdivided to connect smaller swings within the longer trend. The entire price decline from the price high over $60 to the bottom under $15 is viewed as one market swing within the bigger picture or longer-horizon. Within this decline

Figure 1.6   Internal Price Swings in Newmont Mining Stock

there are also shorter-horizon swings. Some move upwards, and some move down. The price action form swings are countertrend moves to the bigger picture of longer-horizon trend. The smaller declines that are marked within Figure 1.6 are smaller price swings *in the direction of the larger trend*. When you are beginning it is always best to trade in the direction of the larger trend.

One might say that the declines connected in this chart are the intermediate trends. When you begin, you want to trade only trends that move in the direction of the larger trend. In this figure the second downswing is much steeper then the first. The second and third are about equally steep compared with each other. The fourth slope line—the one farthest to the right—shows a change: It shows a market running out of steam. The speed is slowing because the slope is not as steep as that of the two preceding downswings. This means that fewer people are selling and the selling pressure is beginning to decrease for the moment. It does not imply a permanent bottom, but it can be read from this slope change that a good bounce upward could develop just from the geometry that was used within the price action.

There are many ways to read a chart to build a story about what is developing within the price data. So far this chapter has described only a few simple ways to make comparisons in a chart. Now it is time to make a quick check of our progress. The purpose of this review is to make you aware that geometry is a necessary aspect of chart reading.

- The slope of a line connecting a price high to a price low can be used to judge the speed of a market decline.

- True or false? A stock that recovers quickly from a prior bear market is viewed as being stronger than a stock that has made the same gains over a longer period of time. [The answer is True.]

Reading Market Trends

You just looked at a method for determining a primary direction for a stock by using swing charts. A swing chart connects the price high and price low of a distinct price movement. There can be very long swings, as you saw in the first chart for Newmont Mining (Figure 1.3) when its internal geometric features were discussed. You also can look at shorter swings, such as the ones in Figure 1.6, where the slope was given consideration. However, the lines do not help you determine when a trend has changed. To do that, more information needs to be added to the chart.

A *swing line* shows the direction and duration of a price move. A trend line connects several price swings to provide a warning that a significant change may be taking place. Figure 1.7 shows a monthly chart for General Motors (GM). This chart was created in 2006, when GM had been in a bear market for more than 6 years. In a downtrend, a *trend line appears above the price decline*. There are two trend lines in Figure 1.7. The accepted definition of a *confirmed* trending market is one in which the price data touched and rebound from the trend line three times. Books about this topic introduce the concept by drawing the lines from a major price high or low. My personal

Figure 1.7 Monthly Chart for General Motors (GM)

experience with trends defining steep slopes suggests that one should establish the trend line in a better place.

Line A in Figure 1.7 is drawn from the price high above the price highs in the downtrend. The price that spikes upward toward point 2 does not touch the trend line. The price swing up to point 3 touches line A. This establishes the trend line, but it is not confirmed until the third time the price action meets the line, which occurs in 2005. By then the steep decline is becoming a historical crash. Consequently, the definition is inadequate.

If you start trend line B just behind the spike high, point 2 establishes the trend and sets an angle that is more meaningful. In this case the definition of a confirmed trend is established much sooner.

The top two bars, or months, at the extreme market high create a specific pattern called a *key reversal*. Some analysts refer to this as a set of railway tracks. The two top bars show how the market advances sharply and cannot sustain the gains. The very next month the market takes away all the gains into the high. This type of pattern is called a *directional signal*. It often leads to a much bigger move, as is shown in Figure 1.7.

If the line over a declining market is considered the trend line and you add a line to the bottoms connecting the price lows, the lower line is only *support*, not the trend. The two are very easy to confuse. In a downtrend, a line added to the price bottoms in addition to the trend line over the price highs forms a channel. It shows the range in which the market trades as it falls. However, there is a catch: If the market breaks either line drawn under the market, it may mean that the current trend is in danger of acceleration (breaking the lower channel) or reversing by exceeding the upper trend line. Therefore, the trend line is a warning line that signifies that the trend could reverse. In the case of a declining market, a reversal requires prices to break above the trend line.

In a rising market, or *bull market*, the trend line is created *under* the price action. Why? If the market breaks down through the trend line, tracking support under the market, it will provide a warning that a major reversal could be developing.

Line A in Figure 1.8 tracks better days for GM from 1994. Note the one horrific meltdown spike through trend line A, which stops just above trend line B. Would you know to draw trend line B before this sharp decline? The truth is that you never would know that trend line B was a confirmed and established trend for GM before the meltdown developed in the market.

The more historical data in Figure 1.9 indicate that GM defined a confirmed trend by early 1995. This was the trend line that the market stopped dead in its tracks at the spike downward into the asterisk symbol (*) under the market. The same trend line

Figure 1.8   Price Rises and Declines for General Motors Stock

became important when the market used it as resistance. Resistance is an inflection price level the market respects by stalling at or impeding the price movement of a rally. The inflection price levels the stop a market decline are called support levels. There is an asterisk in Figure 1.9 to the far right over a price swing high that shows a market failure under a resistance area we discovered using trend lines. The chart also has an asterisk under a sharp decline that stopped right on a trend line marking support. Often a market support level turns into market resistance at a later time. Using trend lines is just one method of finding areas of market support or resistance.

Figure 1.9   Historical Data for General Motors Showing a Confirmed Trend

Why is the second trend line drawn at a higher level from the 1995 low? Because it shows that the market rally is accelerating as the slope of the trend line is becoming steeper.

Figure 1.10 shows a more advanced use of market geometry. The lines radiating upward are created from a single starting price point. In this case, the start of the up trend—when prices begin to move upward with conviction—is illustrated near the start of 1995. The lines have a specified angle between them so that there are no additional price lows and highs. These lines are called *speed lines*. They make it

Figure 1.10   Speed Lines for General Electric Stock to Define Support and Resistance

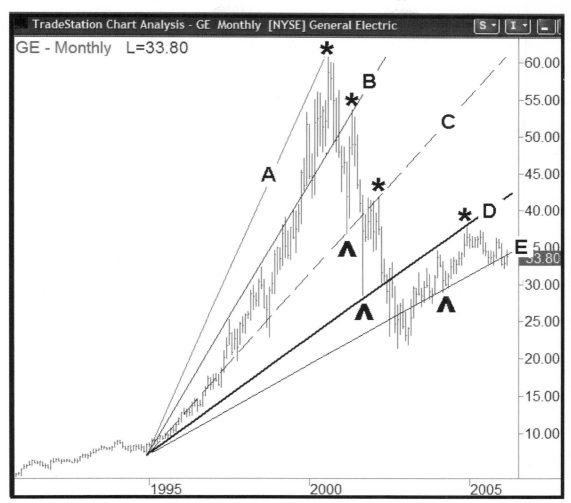

possible to study the ranges in which the market is trading. On the way up, the market is trading between lines B and C most of the time. When GE is trading between lines A and B, the market shows a lot of a back-and-fill action as the prices bars overlap with limited overall gains in the larger trend. This is a warning that the stock is running out of steam.

When the market starts the deep correction, it uses the same lines as support and resistance. The price highs marked with asterisks are testing resistance. The price lows rebounding from the circumflex (^) symbols are testing support. You can see that market geometry became very important from the start of the rally in 1995. The price is starting to break down through line E. That is not a healthy sign, but the tools being used here all contribute to a probability of reaching the best conclusion of the market's direction. As a result, it is premature to form a firm opinion about the health and direction for GE.

Market Movements in Channel Ranges

This chapter has discussed simple trends in a market, but markets tend to move within parallel lines. Figure 1.11 evaluates GE stock in a monthly bar chart. The upward slope defining line B is the trend line. A number 1 is placed at this same point to show it is the first time the market tests this line being drawn. Points 2 and 3 along line B show the second and third time the trend line is respected by the market. Older books on technical analysis will explain the third time a trend line is tested will confirm the trend. Today's markets need this revised and we do this by using other methods to give earlier results. We will add methods such as momentum indicators to give us permission to take action in trends much earlier in a different chapter. Do not forget that up trends are drawn under the price data of a market. Line A is a parallel line that was created by duplicating line B. In this case line A connects two significant highs. The three bars near the start of line D fail to touch the upper line, or channel line A. This is called a *failure,* and it shows that the market has run out of buyers. The market does not break line B[1] until a new downtrend is in force. This configuration provides an excellent way to detect warnings that the market is in the process of making a larger decline.

Often a market will break the lower channel line and then bounce to test the old channel without trading through the lower channel line. In Figure 1.11 GE bounces back through the lower trend line under the rising market swing before making the decline to point 1 on line C. Lines C and D mark the new channel boundaries. Line D, which is drawn above the market, is the new downtrend line. Line C was created from line D by making a parallel duplicate. The new line was then dragged down to connect the bars marked as points 1 and 2. Why was line C not moved to connect the spikes in this downtrend? Points 1 and 2 fit the parallel line earlier than do the major spikes in this decline. Look closely at point 3 on line C. Point 3 holds above the trend line and a line drawn at the extreme spikes that formed earlier would not have been as helpful. Experience will help develop your judgment, but it is always important to understand why you elected to use one

Figure 1.11   Monthly Bar Chart for General Electric (GE)

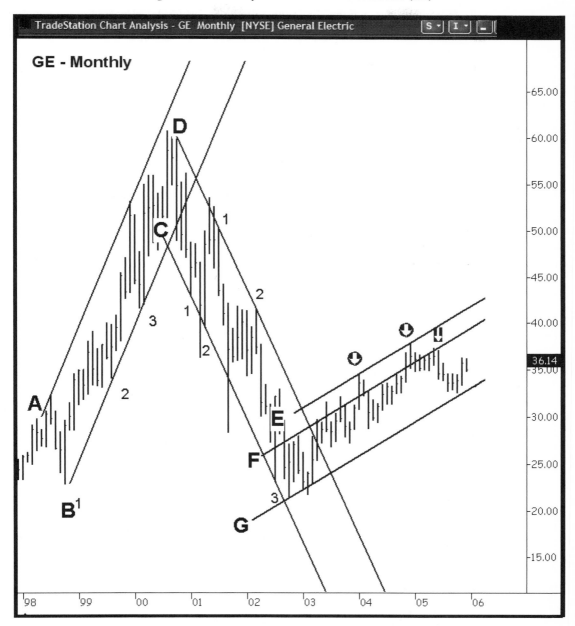

price point rather than another. If you do not know, just paper trade and the market will teach you if you make notes and keep objective to study your results after the market has moved on.

A third parallel line could have been drawn to connect the lows, but you want tools that warn you in advance that a change could be developing. The price bar at point 3 on line C touches the line, and then the market starts a back-and-fill action that fails to touch line C again. When the stock begins to crawl upward, a new channel develops. Lines G and E are fairly easy to follow, but line F connects internal bar highs. Note how many times a bar comes up and stops at line F. It stops seven times before the market fails at the third arrow to the far right. Line F introduces you to the subtle nature of charting, which is not always about the big bold signals. In fact, the more experience you acquire, the more quickly you can detect market trend changes from these subtle internal patterns and signals.

At this point novices usually get so excited about trading that they jump into the fire without having a detailed plan of attack. It is too easy to pick up the phone or enter an order on the Internet. Slow down. The channels that were reviewed in this chapter are not the price objectives. Channels simply indicate when the winds of change are blowing. Chapter 2 will discuss a few trading rules.

Quiz for Chapter 1

1. In 1875, Benner's book *Prophecies of Future Ups and Downs in Prices* did which of the following?
   a. Gave forecast cycles for weather patterns that would affect agriculture
   b. Supplied fundamental reasons why corn market lows occur
   c. Displayed charts to show future market panic highs and lows
   d. Put prices for hogs in historical charts for the first time
   e. Predicted the next bull market in stocks

2. In 1931, Dr Warren Persons, a professor of economics at Harvard University, stated that the underlying cause for business cycles is which of the following?
   a. Human wants, fears, and hope
   b. Supply and demand macroeconomics
   c. Short-term interest rates
   d. Cash flows between emerging markets
   e. Mechanistic world fundamentals

3. In times of economic contraction, a nation often is led out of trouble by which of the following?
   a. Big banks willing to take measured risks to grow remaining large businesses that did not fail
   b. Small businesses and individuals restarting the economy when large banks and business have no interest in assuming new risks
   c. Government easing taxes and reducing stock margins
   d. Government lowering interest rates
   e. Wars

4. Human nature creates patterns in price data that can be measured by which of the following?
   a. Balance and proportional spacing between price swings
   b. Specific pattern formation as human nature repeats the fear and greed cycle
   c. Geometry basics
   d. Growth and decay ratios found in nature
   e. All of the above

5. A line drawn from an internal price swing from market low to a market high will define which of the following?
   a. A market trend
   b. The time required to create the rally
   c. The slope and acceleration of the market swing that is measured
   d. Whether the rally can continue after a small correction
   e. The speed of the market's decline

6. A market directional signal is which of the following?
   a. Confirmation that the larger trend remains strong
   b. A complex pattern developing over time as buyers and sellers slug it out
   c. A signal that requires further confirmation with divergence in momentum indicators
   d. Something that requires immediate consideration by a trader after the market has warned that it is reversing
   e. A signal that forms at a trend line

7. Technical analysis is the study of which of the following?
   a. Human behavior
   b. Measured extremes of sentiment

c. Prices using momentum studies

d. Geometric proportion and balance within price data

e. All of the above

8. A line drawn above a market connecting higher price highs is called which of the following?

a. Support

b. Resistance

c. A trend line at resistance

d. A trend line

e. Support and a trend line

9. A market forms three swings downward, making new price lows from lower highs after a lengthy bear market. When the slopes of the three swings are compared, the slope of each swing is flatter in appearance than the previous one. A technician would interpret this as which of the following?

a. An accelerating bear market about to make another sharp move downward

b. A bull trap in a bear market

c. A weakening bear market preparing to reverse

d. Short sellers taking profits

e. A correction in a bear market

10. Market channels are which of the following?

a. Parallel lines drawn to connect price ranges forming in historical data

b. Order entry paths from a principal broker to the floor

c. Bloomberg, CNBC, MSNBC, and other financial television channels devoted to market news coverage

d. Converging trend lines drawn on the price data

e. Diverging lines drawn on the price data

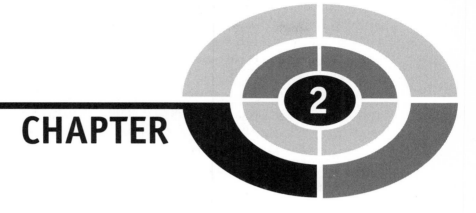

CHAPTER 2

When Do You Trade and How Do You Protect Yourself?

Your Past Personal Baggage Is Your Weak Link

Tiger Woods once said that golf is played on a course that is 6 inches long. He was referring to the space between a golfer's ears. This is true for traders as well. Markets illuminate a trader's strengths and weaknesses. Regardless of skill level, every trader faces demons that will determine his or her success. When traders make a profit, an emotional boost usually follows, but that feeling can become associated too closely with a person's self-image and sense of worth. This is very dangerous. When a losing trade occurs, traders often blame anything and everything around them except themselves; they do not feel accountable for their own actions.

The emotional highs and lows of trading are very polar. One day you are extremely positive about your skill and ability, the next you could be negative about ever having tried as your ego will be battered and bruised. Good traders learn that it is essential to have the discipline to respond to markets without emotion when they are in the act of making, managing, and executing a trade. Only when you do not have a *position on*, or are *flat,* as it is called, can you give yourself permission to feel emotion.

Traders who find themselves thinking in terms of "ifs," "buts," and "could have, would haves" after making an error are in a state of denial. Chill! Every trader makes mistakes, and the market does not make personal attacks. Traders who manage risk correctly will survive to make the next trade. *The market will always be there*. Only you can decide when and how to step into a race that never ends. You are in control of your tools, your selection of a data vendor, and your selection of a market. Be prepared by engaging in disciplined study and offline practice. If you lose, be accountable so that you can make changes and learn.

A great trader named W. D. Gann stepped out of the markets at the high in 1929 and warned those around him that a crash was imminent and that the fall would be a bad one. In one of his courses he made a point that went something like this: "I can give you the best times to enter or exit a position, but if you insist on taking action because of fear or greed, you cannot win."

Ten Rules for Trading

Gann was right, so let me give you a few simple trading rules that will make trading more manageable. These rules and guidelines have been tested by several generations of people brave enough to sit on the front lines.

RULE 1

Never listen to a broker, a neighbor, a friend, or someone you think knows more than you do. It puts you in a position of weakness. Learn to do your own work.

Trade on facts from your own research, not from hope. Hope kills. That's the bottom line.

RULE 2

Never enter an order without making a *stop loss order*. If you trade through a company such as Charles Schwab, you have probably never have had a stop loss order offered to you on the computer screen. They offer it only to those with larger accounts. Go elsewhere if the stop loss order is news to you. A stop loss order shows that you have done your homework. It will identify the price at which you will get out of the market automatically.

If you are *long* (you bought something), a stop loss order is entered under the market entry level. If you are *short* (you sold something you do not own), the stop loss order is entered above the market entry level. When the market trades at or through your price, the stop loss becomes an automatic market order to get out.

If you cannot define where you are wrong, you cannot define the size of the position you are able to establish. You might have a mental stop, but it will be challenged once it is realized. Logic steps in and gives you hundreds of reasons to stay a little longer or revise the mental stop. Human nature allows you to see whatever you want when a position is in trouble. A stop loss order must be entered at the same time you open a position. Do not change it! This is the only way to protect yourself.

RULE 3

Keep a record of your trades; not just the math but the reason you entered a trade. Write the notes immediately. As an example, if you decided to buy the market when the market prices tested one of your trend lines using the methods we covered in Chapter 1, make yourself a note. Use a tape recorder if keeping a log is a pain. Why? After the trade, you will want to see what did not work and what you did right. It is as important to record the good as it is to record the bad. No one wants to have only negative reinforcement. It is also essential to do it at the time the trade is established because you are likely to forget your rationale after the trade is complete.

RULE 4

Be patient. Everything happens more slowly in reality than it does in your mind.

RULE 5

Don't use patience to disguise the fact that you don't know what to do. Give yourself time to learn. Results come slowly, and the curse of novice traders is a quick, fast win. I promise that you will give all your first gains back. Problems will arise from your inability to react to a problem. You will tell yourself that things will get better: If I am *patient*, the market will turn in my favor. But those who are blindly patient wait until near the close or a bottom. That usually puts them in a bigger pickle than they would have been in if they had reacted immediately.

RULE 6

Buck the crowd. Listen to CNBC but don't follow its advice when the air is filled with a tone of excitement. In other words, get out when there is a lot of media hype telling you to jump in. When the world is coming to an end and everybody is in a rush to get out, it's probably time to buy.

RULE 7

Generally, markets discount stocks right after the release of major reports. You win more often by buying when bad news comes out and selling when good news comes out. With the release of major news, the market should react at first in the expected direction. As an example, a negative report should drop the market to aid your timing, while good news should help raise the market. If the market cannot move up on good news, sell fast. If the market cannot move down on bad news, buy fast. Look to your indicators to obtain permission to do this but recognize that when markets have exhausted a trend, they cannot move in the expected direction.

RULE 8

When in doubt, get out immediately. You cannot reassess objectively when the position is on. You must get out in order to reevaluate. If the unknown still exists, stay out. There are three market positions you can be in at any single time: *long*, *short*, and *watching from the sidelines*. The third is the safest and often the smartest position when doubt exists.

RULE 9

It is not necessary to trade constantly. Reread the eighth rule.

RULE 10

Thou shalt not blame thine own failure on the market, your broker, the floor, your lack of concentration that resulted from an interruption, lack of time, poor health, a power failure, your Internet connection, your software, your job, your last seminar, your mother-in-law, your father-in-law, the noise, the heat, the cold, the incorrect news, the lack of sleep, the fear of being left out, or the terrorists. You alone are accountable for your actions as a trader. To be successful, you must take control and be responsible for that control.

The Best Way to Trade

The most money is made by *swing trading*. That means trading with the major trend but focusing on the smaller intermediate trends that are in the direction of the longer-horizon trends. Remember, the longer you hang around, the longer you are exposed to risks. However, this does not mean that you should overtrade. A position held for several days is not overtrading, but if you make four, five, or six trades a day, the cost will eat you alive.

When you are learning, you should not trade on margin. Trading on margin allows you to borrow up to half the cost of a stock from your broker; with futures you can borrow up to 96 percent. Do not do it. Most novice traders do not understand this. Only 6 percent of the people who trade futures win. According to the exchanges, the traders in that 6 percent are taking their profits from the other 94 percent.

The other way to trade is with trailing stops over longer trends, but not as an investment over many years. The current market environment does not support this philosophy, and this statement does not refer exclusively to the buy side. You must be as willing to be short in the market as you are willing to be long.

Qualifications for Success

Here are 10 factors integral to the success of any trader.

1. INDEPENDENCE

First, you must be independent. All good traders do their own work and make their own decisions. Independence is essential because the majority of people are wrong. Consequently, good traders often have a view contrary to the news, the opinions of

their neighbors, and most brokerage firms. They have to step away from everyone so they are not influenced by other's views.

2. A GAME PLAN

It is equally important to have a game plan and stick to it. A successful game plan has three elements: an entry strategy, a get-out-of-trouble strategy, and a winning exit strategy. The game plan goes on to define the correct size to trade on the basis of the first three strategies.

3. KNOWLEDGE

You cannot gain knowledge without taking the time to study. A friend of mine wants to be a trader yet has no time to read a book or set up software with professional features. However, he has the time to establish a few trades. With this mind-set, he'll never be a successful trader. Successful trading requires a commitment to building and cultivating a knowledge base.

4. PATIENCE

Being a patient trader is so hard that this is worth repeating from the discussion earlier in this chapter. It takes patience to wait for trends to be established or to wait for the correct setup to enter. You must have a precise entry level and reason for entering. Jumping in for fear that you'll miss out is not a good enough reason to buy.

5. NERVE

Chuck Yeager was the first pilot to break the sound barrier at Mach 1. When he was asked how he had had the nerve to do it, he replied: "First you do all you can to identify and understand the risks, then you accept your worst possible outcome. After that it is just a matter of stepping into the 'Ugh-known.'" The point is that courage comes from preparation and knowing what you are doing to the best of your ability.

6. GOOD HEALTH

Traders are athletes. You have to train; you must condition yourself to build stamina. If your body is not healthy, your mind becomes mush.

7. TIME

The television is one of the greatest time thieves in existence. If you shut off the television, you will turn to books, your charts, and your computer and focus more clearly for longer periods.

8. KNOWLEDGE OF HUMAN NATURE

A successful trader studies human nature and the mass psychology of crowds. This is called *market psychology*. The majority of popular trends prove to be unreliable and I will give you more detailed guidance in Chapter 11 after you develop your technical skills and apply them. In other words, markets move in the direction that will snag the greatest number of people. There are specific indicators and studies that measure the psychological sentiment of a market. Those indicators help you measure how many people are buying or how many professional or commercial orders are being taken. They also indicate whether the mass public speculator or commercial trader is selling the market. This is valuable information for making successful trades.

In addition to popular trends, there are popular trading prices. Many traders focus on trading in increments of 5, 10, 25, 50, 60, 75, 100, 150, and so forth. Markets hate to sell at even numbers, so keep your orders just shy of these levels. You want to keep your stop orders just short of these round whole numbers as well. If your stop calculation points to 74, make it 73.85. A quick shakeout will pick up the orders that come in at 74 and protect you. If your stop is hit, that constitutes a real washout and you want to be filled. The media made a fuss about the Dow Jones Industrial Average hitting 10,000, but that was just a number. Let your price projection methods define which levels are important and ignore the fascination the mass public has for others.

9. A LIMITED NUMBER OF METHODS

Collecting indicators while in study mode is a big problem for novice traders. Find what works best for you and toss out the others. Keep three non-correlated methods. As you learn about new methods, see how they challenge or improve your old ones. If one is better, toss out an older method. Some people collect so many tools that they become paralyzed and cannot make a decision. (My book *All about Technical Analysis* shows how to develop three non-correlated methods.)

10. DISCIPLINE

The most important quality for successful traders is discipline. It takes discipline to study on a daily basis. It takes discipline to follow the game plan you developed to make a trade. It takes discipline to decide not to fly by the seat of your pants. It is easy to pick up the mouse or phone and enter an order, but you've skipped the steps needed to prepare. Without discipline, it is impossible to trade successfully.

Different Kinds of Markets

CREEPING MARKETS

A market that has low volume and few swings keeps creeping along slowly until suddenly it makes a fast run, at that point traders who didn't pay attention are on the wrong side or are left out. Don't go against a slow creeping vine. The early stages of longer-horizon bull swings and bear swings often begin in this manner. Take into consideration the fact that traders around the world are wired together. This synergy develops into certain market traits because there is little time for people to be enticed into the slow creep or to be forced out because of positions held on the wrong side.

FAST MARKETS

A fast market may occur when there is a sudden meltdown in stocks after specific news comes out. As a rule, never chase a fast market. If you are left out, walk away from the computer and wait until the market defines a bounce on another day. I have made higher profits by trading the final swings than by being in the first fast move. That is the case because there are strong, confident levels to buy or sell into and the risk can be defined clearly.

SIDEWAYS MARKETS

A sideways market, or one that is directionless, should be avoided. Patience is the key here because you have to wait for the market to confirm its intent. If you start making trades out of boredom, you will not be around long enough to trade the larger move that follows.

Back to the Original Question: When Do You Trade and How Do You Protect Yourself?

Trade when there is a market at a precise target level and your indicators give you permission to take action. Protect yourself by always using stop loss orders, and remember that they must be entered at the time you enter the trade. Chapter 11 will discuss various order types.

Quiz for Chapter 2

1. When a trader has no positions in the market, that trader is said to be:
   a. Undecided
   b. Watching
   c. Flat
   d. On vacation

2. You just established a position in a stock and discovered that you made an error. The best thing to do is:
   a. Cover the position immediately
   b. Yell about the fill to improve your odds
   c. Wait a few moments so that you can check other indicators quickly to clarify whether an error was made
   d. Enter an order double of a size that reverses the original position

3. One of the hardest things for new traders to learn is:
   a. A stop should be used only in slow markets
   b. The market is always there, and there is no finish line
   c. When to add to a trade that is in trouble
   d. When to exit a winning trade

4. One of the hardest things for new traders to accept is the fact that
   a. Data vendors can be wrong in some of the technical indicators they offer
   b. They have to be accountable for their own actions at all times
   c. A and B

5. It is just as important for traders to know the price level the market will move toward as to know the price level at which their opinion is wrong.

   a. Beginners learn price projection when they are more advanced and have experience trading

   b. False

   c. True

   d. Price projection is important, but it is not possible to be exact

6. A stop loss order should be entered:

   a. When you trade stocks

   b. When you trade futures

   c. After the first swing under a moving average

   d. When you enter the original order

   e. After the market moves off the trend line

7. One of the most difficult things for any trader is to do is:

   a. Be right more than 80 percent of the time

   b. Accept the fact that you cannot control the market

   c. Recognize that most market moves happen more slowly than you think they will happen

   d. Learn to accept big drawdowns in your capital

   e. Learn how to trade 24-hour markets and get enough sleep

8. The media are best used by traders to:

   a. Hear the results of the Federal Open Market Committee meetings

   b. Fade or buck the crowd

   c. Keep in touch with breaking news events concerning earnings reports

   d. Identify overlooked buy and sell stock recommendations

   e. Obtain international market data

9. A stock has been declining, with expectations that bad news will soon be announced by the company. You have a short position on when your suspicions are proved correct. The market reacts by opening with an extreme gap downward that exceeds your target price considerably. You should immediately do which of the following?

   a. Add to your wining position

   b. Do nothing and quickly calculate where the new target price will be below your first target

c. Take a third of the position off and move the stop down to the price level at which you entered the short trade

    d. Do nothing and determine where resistance will form to add to the position

    e. Immediately take profits

10. Most money is made when a position follows which of the following?

    a. A failure in a directional pattern

    b. A sharp countertrend bounce that catches the majority of traders off balance

    c. High market volatility in leveraged options

    d. The longer-horizon trend

    e. A string of small winning trades

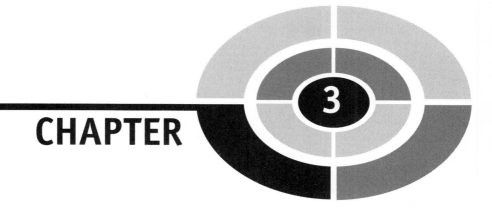

Which Price Levels Are Important?

Trend Lines

The figures in Chapter 1 showed how to draw a simple trend line and explained how a trend line *drawn under a rising market* can become market support. Chapter 1 also showed how a trend line drawn *above a declining market* can define market resistance. These lines mark important price levels, but most market action develops away from these simple trend lines. Even when you add parallel lines to a trend to create a channel as we did in Figure 1.11 for the stock GE, you will need other methods to determine important price levels that the markets will respect.

It is important to know that markets do not move in perfectly symmetrical swings. This may sound confusing at first. Every price swing, whether low or high, will have a proportional relationship to another swing that is on the same chart. The smaller price swings also may have mathematically proportional ratios that are related to the larger price trend. The better you are at identifying those relationships, the more accurate you will be at forecasting future price movements. Later in this chapter you will discover that markets move up and down in accordance with mathematical constants known as *universal constants*.

Fortunately, markets have periods in which they move in very symmetrical ways. As a novice trader you will have great success during those periods, but be aware that that success will not last if your methods do not improve because the market will revert to an expanding or contracting cycle as part of its natural evolution. If you do not have the tools to accommodate those market changes, you will give back all the gains you made when the markets moved in simple symmetrical proportions.

Calculating Support Levels

Figure 3.1 is a monthly chart for Computer Associates. Use the following method for calculating support levels: From the price low to the price high (before 1999), subdivide this range into eight equal parts. The sharp correction that follows passes through five of those sub-ranges. Each line is a support line that is important. How do you know the market will decline through four lines? Simply drawing lines on a chart will not help you identify which range is more important. Technical analysis is not only about the tool you select to use but also about how you apply it.

Look at the prices that fall on the lines in the figure. You will see that the market respects, that is, reacts to, only one support line in its history within this range. The sharp decline that bottomed near the line labeled 24.241 is of far greater importance than any of the declines above it. Remember, that price pivot low was on the chart when the price range was subdivided. If you look more closely, you will see that the stock tested this line of support one other time as well. You are learning to read individual stock charts to determine what is important to that unique set of market data rather than applying a fixed rule. This is an important mind-set that you must adopt. Discover what each individual chart is trying to tell you. Do not twist the meaning by learning a particular technique and forcing it on the market.

Figure 3.1   Subdividing a Price Range: Monthly Bar Chart for Computer Associates (CA)

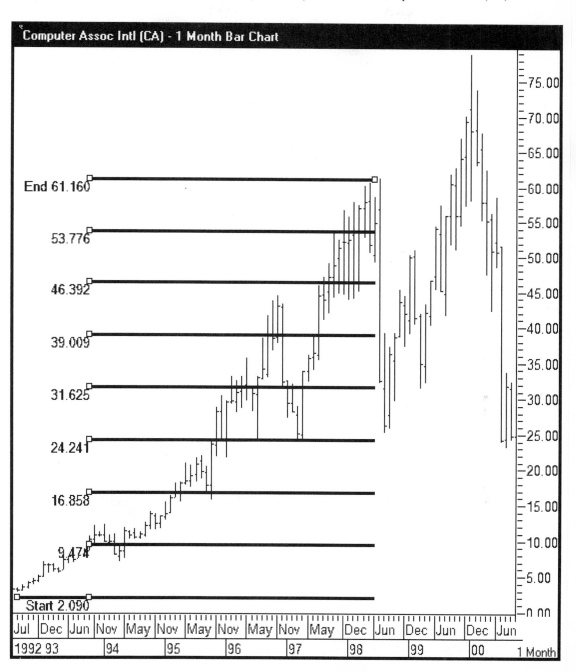

The monthly chart shown in Figure 3.1 respects one price subdivision or support zone with great results, but the price action within the range seems to blow right through the lines that have been drawn there. (I am not referring to the data to the right of the range that has been divided, only to the data contained within the range.)

Because all the pivots within the range do not respect the lines that were drawn, this is the first warning that something else is developing. Another method is needed to indicate whether the market will break the line, or you need to reconsider how you subdivided the entire price swing.

Before removing the lines that subdivide the range shown in Figure 3.1, look at the most recent data in Figure 3.2 that is plotted on the far right. The subdivisions have been extended to the right. You will find that the price pivots marked with asterisks are still respecting the ranges created from the data from 1992 to 1998. In fact, after the big break formed in 1998, you can see that the support line above it was tested again during a sharp drop in 1999. The second break is a warning to an experienced technician that the price lines should not be removed because the price swings are proportional.

But what about the rally from 1998 into the historical price high?

To analyze Figure 3.3, begin by subdividing the price range from a price low to a price high. In this chart, the 1998 price low marks the start (labeled S) and the historical high marks the range you want to divide into eighths. Look closely at the decline that follows the historical high. The market bounces up into the underside of the lines where asterisks are drawn. Here support lines have become lines of resistance. Furthermore, as time goes on in the more recent data, the market is respecting the *same resistance lines*. However, the lines you extended to the right are subdividing a price range that is totally different from the range that began at the 1998 low and ended at the market's historical high. The other range you should subdivide into eighths is the price swing from 1992 to the high before the 1998 decline as demonstrated in Figure 3.2.

Markets indeed have a proportional relationship in size within the price swings that follow. As your study continues, you will discover that markets have harmonic relationships as well.

The methods used to analyze markets are mathematically driven and logically applied in a consistent manner, but you can get a far deeper understanding if you dig deeper. For example, why did I suggest subdividing the range into eighths rather than sixths? The answer is complicated. The proportions go back to the time of the ancient Greek Pythagoreans and sacred geometry, both of which continue to have significance for traders.

Figure 3.2   Monthly Chart for Computer Associates (CA)

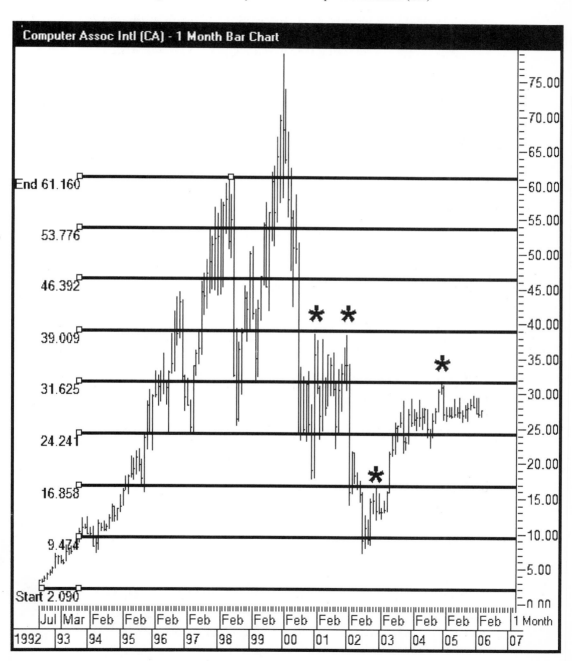

Figure 3.3   Resistance Within the Monthly Chart for Computer Associates (CA)

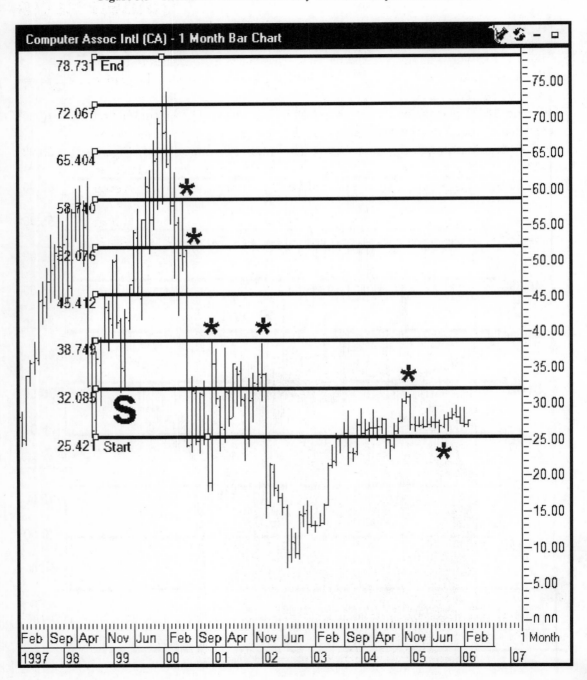

The Golden Ratio

Pythagoras was credited with discovering a universal proportional constant in the year 580 BC that you will apply to your charts. The constant is referred to by the Greek letter *phi* and is called the Golden Ratio. The numerical value of the golden ratio is 161.8 percent.

The ratio 161.8 percent or the number 1.618 is an expansion or contraction constant that is found everywhere in nature. When there is a growth and decay cycle, this ratio mathematically describes it. The spiral of a seashell (see Figure 3.4), the spiral of a hurricane, and the spiral of our Solar System all have an expansion ratio or mathematical relationship of 1.618. This ratio is called a Universal Constant.

The 1.618 ratio was discovered in 580 BC by Pythagoras, but it is the Italian mathematician Leonardo Fibonacci's famous number series 0, 1, 1, 2, 3, 5, 8, 13,

Figure 3.4   A Fibonacci Spiral in Nature

21, 34, 55, 89, 144, and so on to infinity, with which that ratio is most closely associated. Look at this number's unique properties and you will see how to apply it in a market context. The value 1.618 is immensely important, as is its reciprocal, 0.618. It does not matter whether you multiply, divide, subtract, or add these numbers; the result will always be a Fibonacci ratio.

For example, if you multiply:

$$0.618 \times 0.618 = 0.382$$
$$0.382 \times 0.618 = 0.236$$
$$0.236 \times 0.618 = 0.146$$

If you subtract:

$$1.000 - 0.618 = 0.382$$
$$0.618 - 0.382 = 0.236$$
$$0.382 - 0.236 = 0.146$$

This is also true for the following equation:

$$1.618 \times 1.618 = 2.618$$
$$2.618 \times 1.618 = 4.236$$

Therefore, if you use the Fibonacci ratios 61.8 percent, 50 percent, and 38.2 percent, or 0.618, 0.50, and 0.382, you will be able to calculate any of the other Fibonacci ratios illustrated above just by making several projections. (There is a detailed study of the Fibonacci ratio in my book *All About Technical Analysis*. Refer to that work if you want to know what is behind the methods presented here.)

Applying Fibonacci's Ratios

The stock price of the home builder Hovnanian Enterprises (HOV) is shown in Figure 3.5. The price data are subdivided into the proportions 38.2 percent, 50 percent, and 61.8 percent. The golden ratio is 61.8 percent. It is important to recognize that 38.2 percent and 61.8 percent are the same displacement from the nearest outer border of the range being subdivided. Now look at Figure 3.6 and measure the distance from the 38.2 percent line to point A, and the distance from the 61.8 percent line and point B. They are the same length.

Figure 3.5   Monthly Bar Chart for Hovnanian Enterprises (HOV)

Figure 3.6

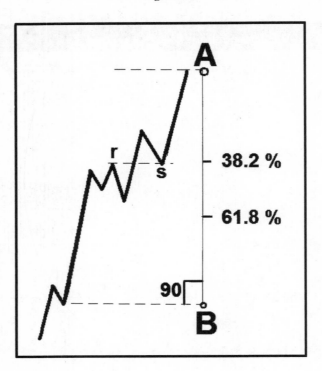

Study the subdivisions in Figure 3.5 closely. I have not taken the price high or the extreme low as the defined range to subdivide. The most important pivot is rarely the price high or low but the secondary swing that follows the extreme. Why? The high ends the uptrend, and the high of the bar beside it marks the start of the new downtrend. The second pivot is the one of greatest value, according to W. D. Gann, an early market forecaster and trader mentioned in Chapter 2. (Although some of his methods are exceedingly advanced, some of the basics behind those methods can help you avoid novice errors now.) This explains why the high is not the start of the range; but why was the price low in the middle of the rally that was selected?

First, look at the price data and find the strongest price bar in the trend. In this chart it falls within the swing that begins at around $15 and ends near $35. To find a price retracement, start from the price high. If you start from the low and work up from there, as most people do, you will not see the reaction to the ratios that have been drawn to the left in the prices. If you divide a range using a low near $15, the internal price highs and lows run through the subdivisions of 61.8 percent, 50 percent, and 38.2 percent. Therefore, move the price low up to the first low that allows the old data to stop just at or below those division lines. In 2003 there is a major price high near $49 right under the 38.2 percent line. Earlier that year there is a major price high near $35 that falls just under the 61.8 percent line.

This is what you are looking for because what the market respected in the past, it will respect in the future. Note the more recent decline and then note how it bounced upward off the 50 percent line. If you had used this tool without thinking and selected the range by using the price high and low, the market would not have stopped at your support lines. Why? This is a market that is in an expansion cycle. If it were moving in a simple linear manner, the first method would have worked; however, in an expansion cycle, the swings are longer in each move upward and the declines are shallow because the proportional ratios are shifting upward. What you need to understand is that it is not sufficient to snap a tool onto the chart without thought. You must consider it and *let the market tell you what the right choice is*. Identifying the right choice entails knowing and understanding that the market respected those proportional lines in the past.

Applying a Second Set of Measurements

Figure 3.7 shows the prices of the HOV stock in a monthly bar chart. A second range has been defined and subdivided into the proportions 38.2 percent, 50 percent, and 61.8 percent. The start always is viewed as zero, and the end always is valued as 100. In Figure 3.5 you started from near the historical price high. In Figure 3.7 use the same starting price high for the second measurement. However, this time the ending point is the price low near $23.50. It is the low marked with the second question mark. Why choose this low? Because it is a low that starts one of the strongest upswings in the entire rally. When this second range is subdivided, you will see two lines fall on top of each other at 41.37 and 41.95. These two price levels are very close to one another and reveal a major area of price support for the stock HOV. (The zone is highlighted in the black box in the center of the chart.)

Note that one of the lines is a 50 percent retracement from the first range; the line that overlaps it is a 61.8 percent retracement that was taken from a *different* range. The overlap reveals major support, and you can see from the chart that the market has respected the price zone in this area. The heavy S under this key area means 'S' for support, not 'S' for sell. The price pivots marked r and s indicate

Figure 3.7 Monthly Bar Chart for Hovnanian Enterprises (HOV)

where the market shows resistance to and support for these calculations. These smaller tests at these levels should give you confidence that you have done this calculation correctly.

Adding a Momentum Indicator

Figure 3.8 includes a simple 14-period relative strength index (RSI) applied under the data. This technical study is called a *momentum indicator*. It helps determine when markets are overbought or oversold. When the indicator is at an extreme high,

Figure 3.8   Hovnanian Enterprises with a Relative Strength Index (RSI)

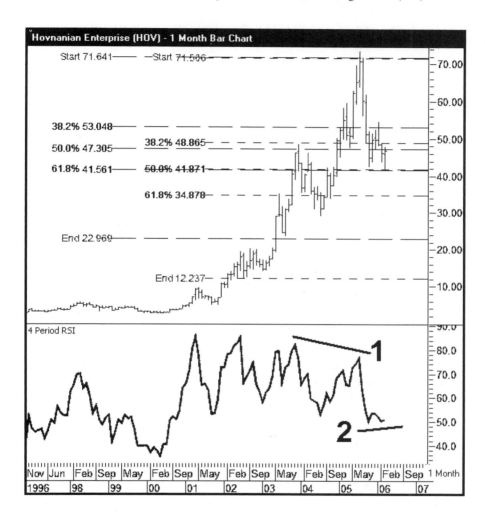

it shows a market that is overextended from buying activity. When the indicator is at extreme lows, this shows that sellers have extended their exuberance as well. In this chart the momentum pattern at line 2 is a buy signal, and so the indicator gives you permission to buy near your target zone. (The mistake most people make is to use these studies without any price objective in mind.)

Remember, the market should not break your major support zone, so be sure to position a stop loss order close under that zone. You know how much you have at risk and have a good idea that the bounce can run to the next zone. Now you have collected the minimal facts needed to make a trade.

Quiz for Chapter 3

1. A line drawn above a market connecting lower highs is called which of the following?

   a. Support

   b. A trend line and resistance

   c. Resistance

   d. A trend line

   e. Support and a trend line

2. A line drawn above a market that connects higher price highs is called which of the following?

   a. Resistance

   b. Support

   c. A trend line at resistance

   d. A trend line

   e. Support and a trend line

3. Small price swings often have the following relationship to the larger market swing:

   a. A mathematical relationship

   b. A proportional harmonic ratio

   c. An internal pattern that mirrors the larger picture in a symmetrical manner

   d. A mathematical relationship to the range of price swings that preceded the move

   e. All of the above

4. The number 1.618 is called:

   a. The golden mean

   b. Phi

   c. The golden ratio

   d. phi

   e. A, B, and C

5. The Fibonacci number series is:

   a. 0, 1, 2, 3, 6, 12, etc.

   b. 0, 1, 1, 2, 3, 5, 8, etc.

   c. 1, 1, 2, 4, 8, 16, etc.

   d. $0.618 \times 1, 0.618 \times 2, 0.618 \times 3, 0.618 \times 5$, etc.

   e. 0, 1, 1, 1, 3, 5, 9, 17, etc.

6. When you add, subtract, multiply, or divide Fibonacci ratios, you obtain which of the following?

   a. An irrational number

   b. A prime number

   c. Another Fibonacci ratio

   d. A value of 1.618

   e. A and C

7. In creating Fibonacci retracements, always do which of the following?

   a. Start from a price low

   b. Start from a price high to find resistance

   c. Start from a price low to find resistance

   d. Start from a price high to find support

   e. C and D

8. When you are buying the market, place a stop loss order:

   a. Over the market at the same time as the original order

   b. At the market to establish the trade

   c. Over the market to create a stop entry order into a trade

   d. Under the market at the same time as the original order

   e. Later to exit a losing trade

9. A common error made in using a proportional divider to subdivide a price range is to:

   a. Measure the diagonal spread between the price high and the price low

   b. Measure from the price high to the price low using a 90-degree angle

   c. Set the middle pin holding the tool together at 10 instead of 6

   d. Measure from a price low to a price high using a 90-degree angle

   e. Measure only a secondary swing within a larger price move

10. The ratio 1.618 can be found in which of the following?

    a. Beethoven's Fifth Symphony

    b. A sunflower

    c. A ratio between the Sun, the Earth, and Venus

    d. The Great Pyramid of Giza

    e. All of the above

CHAPTER 4

When Is a Market Overbought or Oversold?

The Extremes of Public Sentiment

"If your barber and mailman are talking about their stock winners, it's time to run and take cover." This Wall Street saying means that it is impossible for the majority to be right. The first rule about an overbought market is that it can become even more overbought. Internet stocks continually pushed the NASDAQ Index to highs that actually locked or froze the movement of the indicator at extremes for months. When the NASDAQ topped in March 2000, the crash that followed was anticipated by many traders because the aftermath of that kind of market exuberance had been seen before.

Technical Analysis Demystified

Figure 4.1 shows two 2-month bar charts. The NASDAQ is on the left, and Japan's stock index, the Nikkei, is on the right. The markets look very similar, though the Nikkei topped and crashed in 1990, nearly 10 years before the NASDAQ did. When mass public sentiment runs amok with greed, this is the result. This is an extreme case that rarely skips a whole generation because the lessons of the past are easily forgotten.

Figure 4.1   The NASDAQ and the Nikkei

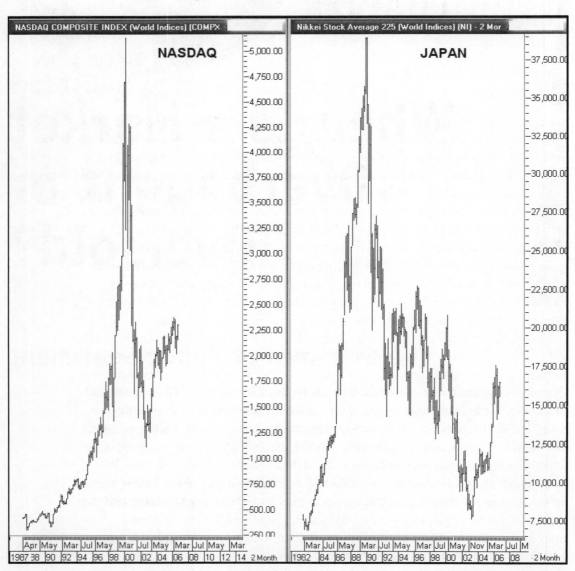

Chapter 1 discussed a 1931 statement by the economics professor Dr. Warren M. Persons:

The world of affairs in which we live is not a mechanistic world; it is a bewildering world of multiplicities, complexities, interactions, repercussions and the vagaries of human wants, fears and hopes. It is a world in which, at times, facts and logic become subordinated to human emotions. At such times individuals, who by themselves are rational, join with other rational individuals to form an unreasoning mob.

Reading Indicators

We can measure the sentiment of the masses. The charts of the Nikkei and NASDAQ shown in Figure 4.1 provide proof that the extremes have occurred and will occur again in the future. But how is it possible to measure mass behavior and determine when it is at extremes and when it is only exhibiting normal day-to-day ranges? The key to reading the indicators successfully is to use them in conjunction with multiple time frames. For example, Figure 4.1 is a 2-month bar chart. If you put oscillators on the data, you will paint one picture. To increase your probability of success, it is important to study weekly and daily charts as well. If all these time frames paint the same picture, that constitutes a compelling argument for buying or selling a stock.

Not only do oscillators warn you about irrational extremes, they can give you an indication of what will happen at the price targets you have identified. However, I recommend that you do not use them alone to create trading signals.

All momentum indicators have the same underlying concept: Compare the close today with the close a particular number of days ago to see if today is stronger or weaker. You can get fancy with this concept and toss in variations on the same theme. One formula shows comparisons across market highs divided by a range of lows. Another indicator will massage and weight today's results across a range of weighted market sessions. Weighting means that the most recent trading sessions are given greater importance than are the days that have faded into history. All these methods produce similar information.

Figure 4.2A shows a weekly chart for the stock of Best Buy (BBY). First, focus on the lines above the price data at the top of the chart. There are two lines, and the heavier black line is squigglier than the second line, which is fairly steady. Both lines are moving averages of closing prices. The lines were created by defining a look-back period, or range for study. In this chart the heavy black line takes a look

Figure 4.2A   Weekly Chart for Best Buy (BBY) with RSI

at 21 weekly bars. The closing prices are added together, and the result is divided by the number of periods in the range to determine an average. As a new week begins, the oldest week drops out of the average. That is why the line mapped on the data is called a *moving average*.

The two averages shown in Figure 4.2A have different look-back ranges in their calculations. One uses 21 periods, and the other uses 125 periods. The greater amount of data in the range causes the second line to be smoother or move more slowly because more data is used to create an average. Longer-period moving averages are also slow to react to market changes: When you look at the 21-period moving average, it has more movement. These averages help you identify market trends. The price data through 2003 stay above the heavy line: the 21-period moving average. Eventually the market breaks that line near the end of 2003 and makes a choppy correction into a low in 2004. Note that the price low in 2004 does not break below the second moving average.

A longer-period average can be considered the market's intermediate trend, and a shorter-period average can be thought of as an indicator of a short trend. These tools can be used on any chart and with any time horizon. However, they lag behind the real market tops and bottoms. They also have a tendency to create confusion when the market swings upward through the line and breaks back through over a period of time. That is called being whipsawed to death. It costs you a lot of money if you have only these tools to work with in making trading decisions. How can you solve these problems?

THE OSCILLATOR EXTREME

Take a look at the second window under the price data in Figure 4.2A, which I call the *oscillator extreme*. It is calculated by subtracting the shorter-period average plotted on price from the longer-period average to create a single number that shows the spread between those two averages. When the two averages cross, the difference is zero because they are both the same. When the shorter-period average is below the longer-period average, the result is a negative number. When the shorter-term average swings higher than the long-term average, there is a positive spread.

In the oscillator extreme frame, the spread between the 125-period and 21-period averages discussed above is plotted. In this window it can be seen that a spread greater than 10 is rare for the time period in this chart. The oscillator crosses the zero line only twice. It drops down into the negative area below zero when the shorter-period average falls in 2002. The oscillator crosses up through the zero line when the short average breaks above the longer-horizon period. This method of tracking the spread between two averages is called *detrending*. It takes the averages that are moving freely with

price and provides a way to map them in a more confined space as a displacement above and below zero. They can move as far away from zero as they want, and the chart scale will change to accommodate the movement. What if you do not want them to move freely but prefer that they stay in a contained range? It is easier to track extremes and make historical comparisons when the indicators track in a fixed range.

THE RELATIVE STRENGTH INDEX

The frame nearest the bottom of Figure 4.2A has an oscillator called the *relative strength index* (RSI). The formula is not that important, but the concept of why it exists and the correct way to read it are significant. When you compare the averages plotted as a detrended line and the RSI at the bottom of the chart, you can see that the foundations for both studies must have common roots. It is also clear that both methods lag behind the market turns. Both methods make comparisons over a price range and then plot the results. The RSI is a little fancier because it includes comparisons in the price highs and lows. The RSI, however, has much more squiggle room in the path it takes.

Note that the RSI does not extend beyond the zero line or the 100 line. A formula that is forced to stay within this fixed boundary has been normalized. The mathematics behind the indicator prevents it from ever having a value less than zero or greater than 100. When you examined the spread between the two averages, you only plotted the value. This entails using a method that has not been normalized. Both systems have advantages and weaknesses.

Like Figure 4.2A, Figure 4.2B is a weekly chart for Best Buy. One of the ways to use the RSI is to watch when it moves in a divergent direction relative to the price data. There are lines in this chart that compare price highs and lows with the RSI within similar time frames. In each pairing, the price highs and lows make new highs and new lows when the indicator (RSI) does not. The study of this conflicting movement between price and oscillator is called *divergence analysis*.

When the market makes a new high but the RSI stays flat or declines, the two lines diverge. When the market makes a new low and the oscillator swings make higher lows, these small trend lines are converging. When the discrepancy develops with market highs, the signal is called *bearish divergence*. When the discrepancy develops at the market lows, the signal is called *bullish divergence*. Because the lines are pointing together, why is it not called it *bullish convergence*? Both are divergence signals, but one is really a convergence signal, and it is bullish for the market.

Can all divergence signals be given the same amount of attention? There is a consideration you should make in regard to the signal: How much time separates the peaks? For example, the bearish divergence signal on the far right side of Figure 4.2B

Figure 4.2B   Divergence Analysis for Best Buy (BBY)

is a bona fide pattern, but it is too wide and has taken too much time. Often the same signal will form again in a tighter pattern that offers a higher probability. The higher probability means you are being given confirming information about the market's plans ahead. However, this chart shows that the signal was correct, as the market declined toward $45 after the divergence developed. It worked this time, but you cannot have high confidence that it will work the same way the next time. Signals with tighter formations have a better probability of being right. That is why technical analysis is a study of odds. You always want the odds to be in your favor.

If you want the best odds for success, you need the best tools. Is the RSI oscillator the best tool to use for divergence analysis?

THE STOCHASTIC OSCILLATOR

Figure 4.2C utilizes the weekly chart of BBY to make another comparison. The spread of two moving averages has been removed, and an oscillator called the Stochastic Oscillator has been placed in the middle frame under the price data. One of my mentors, the late George Lane, developed the Stochastic Oscillator. His indicator is perhaps the one that is used most widely by traders. When you compare his oscillator with the RSI developed by Welles Wilder, you will see many similarities. You also will see that the Stochastic Oscillator swings move more frequently to the outer ranges confined to zero and 100. The rally in 2003 shows the Stochastic Oscillator locking near the highs.

This is very common with normalized formulas. Every time the locked indicator declined a little off its highs, there was another opportunity to buy into the stock rally. Many books and vendors advise traders to sell when the Stochastic Oscillator drops down through an 80 level *or* to buy when it moves up through the 20 level. (Look at the *y* axis to see the indicator value.) This is bad advice and will cost you a considerable amount of money because markets do not end these longer trends the first time the indicator reaches the top or bottom of its range.

Which Indicator Do You Prefer?

The history of an indicator is determined by the probability that something will happen at the same indicator level that was formed previously. If the market respects a certain signal and keeps doing so in the same time period, do not let anyone tell you differently. Beginners need fixed patterns to learn the basics, but fixed patterns such as always looking at the extremes suggest that that is the only piece of information available. Technical analysis is as much an art as it is a science. Learn to read your charts from

Figure 4.2C   Weekly Chart for Best Buy (BBY) with Stochastic and RSI Oscillators

right to left to see if a specific market or stock respects a certain pattern setup. Does it need to retest old momentum highs a couple of times? Does the market give only one warning that a bottom is forming by making a sharp V pattern? Or do you find that the indicator needs a slower, more complex formation? Answering these questions is the best way to learn.

RSI OR THE STOCHASTIC OSCILLATOR?

I prefer the RSI because the indicator movement is cleaner than it is with the Stochastic Oscillator. I always use a 14-period interval with RSI because it has a characteristic that the Stochastic Oscillator does not have. In Figure 4.2C, all the indicator highs bounce up toward 80 in the RSI. The lows from 2004 to 2006 all stay above 40. When the market is defining a bull market rally, the corrections will allow the RSI to stay above 35 to 40. That is important to know. When the rally begins again, the indicators run toward a level over 70. In a bear market, when prices are falling, the RSI tends to top out near 65 and the market resumes the decline, pushing the RSI well below the 40 level. This range comparison can be very useful when a correction prompts you to ask whether the market is experiencing a bear market or a bull market.

The Stochastic Oscillator cannot give you this information, but it can give you different important information. The indicator is set up using half the period of a cycle. (See Chapter 8 for a detailed discussion of cycles.) The Stochastic Oscillator has an advanced method of giving a price projection by measuring the price action relative to the momentum action between the upper and lower boundaries. This is a more advanced technique than you may be ready for at the moment, but it helps explain why analysts have their favorites. Each indicator is a little different, and some traders would not want to be caught without the edge they think their indicator provides relative to others.

In Figure 4.2C, two vertical lines are drawn upward from the momentum lows in the RSI indicator. One is found with the low in 2002, and the other is marked at the momentum low in 2005. In the first, the Stochastic Oscillator creates what is called a *flutter pattern* near the lows when the RSI actually is diverging with prices as a bottom forms. Look at the signal in 2005: The RSI displays no divergence, but it is testing the momentum low in the middle of the range that formed in 2004. The Stochastic Oscillator tests the bottom, but the visual difference is more extreme because the swings cover a wider range. The Stochastic Oscillator makes what is called a *double bottom*. I like the cleaner pattern in the RSI, but it may be more difficult to see the same pattern in it because most traders do not look to the left to read the history of an indicator.

Figure 4.2D   Weekly Chart for Best Buy (BBY) with Moving-Average Convergence
Divergence Oscillator (MACD)

MOVING-AVERAGE CONVERGENCE DIVERGENCE

Take another look at the stock of Best Buy in Figure 4.2D. Between the Stochastic Oscillator and RSI indicators there is a new momentum oscillator called *moving-average convergence divergence* (MACD). This indicator maps two moving-average formulas and their difference, or *spread*, in the same frame. The vertical bars at the bottom of the page help you compare the three oscillators at the same points in time.

In comparison to the RSI and the Stochastic Oscillator, these lines are smooth and turn less frequently. It is for this reason that people like these indicators and use them with the RSI or the Stochastic Oscillator to show longer-horizon trends. However, there is a catch: Referring to the same vertical line used on the RSI in 2002 and 2005, take a look at how slow the MACD is to change direction, allowing the faster average to cross up over the slower average. It was nearly 2 months late in 2002 and about 3 weeks late in 2005. As soon as you smooth out the squiggles, you begin to lag even farther behind the market changes. A way to solve this problem is to use one indicator to exit the market and a faster setup or a faster indicator to exit the market and protect profits. That way, you will have a few ways to improve your odds of being correct.

Momentum indicators are of tremendous value but have a horrible track record for providing the exact time to enter or exit a trade. Technicians use many more indicators, but the truth is that most indicators do exactly the same thing. It comes down to individual preference. Do you want lots of squiggles to warn you that something is about to change or a two-by-four over the head that means you may have to do something immediately? I tend to like something in the middle.

Divergence

The Best Buy weekly chart in Figure 4.2B introduced you to bearish and bullish divergence. The last signal formed with pivots in 2005 and 2006. This bearish divergence signal is a lower probability because it is viewed very wide. The chart shows a very deep retracement back toward the high developed that further demonstrates this last divergence signal was too early. When there is bearish divergence between price and a momentum indicator, it is a warning that the move is running out of steam. The tighter the formation of the signal, the sooner the signal will be respected by the market.

Here are some important points about divergence:

1. Divergence does not mean that the larger trend has ended. It only warns you that the current move is waning.

2. Divergence does not indicate what type of trend reversal will occur. Either a sharp deep trend reversal or a slow coiling price pattern that takes time to consolidate in a sideways range could form. You will never know what will develop by looking at a momentum indicator alone.

3. Most important, a divergence pattern is not a trade signal by itself until it develops at one of the price levels you have defined as support or resistance. The signal is a clear sign for the purpose of analysis, but traders need signals with higher probability and better timing since money is at stake.

Many people will debate the third point above, but most traders have no idea how to define an exact price level where the market is going as a trading target. Even fewer can tell you where the market should not go. Many professional traders fall into the second category. The seminars I give focus on price and time since few traders have methods to address these questions. After experiencing a few losses, most novices become motivated to learn more and eventually agree that a divergence pattern is not a signal by itself. It is easier to accept up front that price targets have to be defined in terms of where the market is going and then study the indicator to see if you have permission to take action.

Grading the Indicators

If a divergence signal is important, it is helpful to know how to grade the strength of the warning. When more factors point to a confirmation, that often increases the probability that the divergence will be correct. Looking more closely at the ways to grade the indicator is important. The first way to grade the indicator is to evaluate how much time the signal took to form. In the case of Best Buy, the last bearish divergence signal was extremely wide.

Figure 4.3 is a weekly chart for Intel (INTC). Under the price data it shows the oscillator MACD. Refer to the double lines swinging over and under the zero line in the following discussion. There are two lines because a second line has been added to smooth the first calculation even more.

Figure 4.3   Weekly Chart for Intel

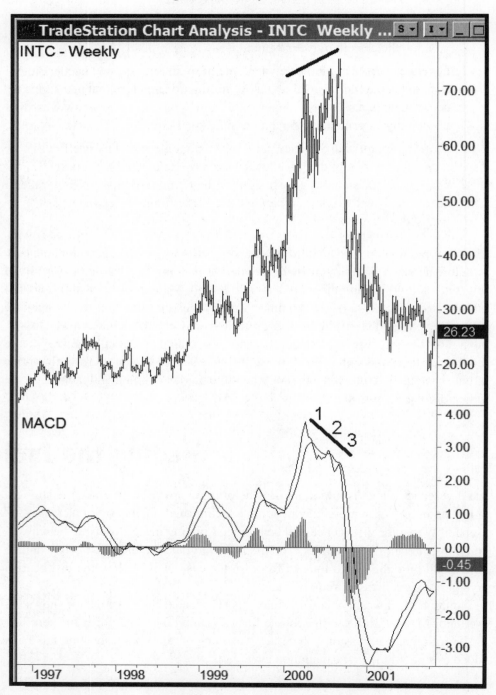

The chart shows three declining momentum peaks as prices made new highs into the historical highs of 2000. The first signal occurs when divergence is present with price at peak 2. When you are using this indicator, wait for the third peak. The first signal has a lower probability of being right than does the signal that offers confirmation in peak 3. This is one way to grade the strength of the signal. Are multiple divergences forming the signal? When that is the case, the repeating signal is always more important.

Figure 4.4 shows prices and the Stochastic Oscillator diverging. This example illustrates that the signal does not necessarily have to develop at historical price highs to be correct. The Stochastic Oscillator indicator makes three peaks, and they form nearly at the same displacement highs that developed at the highs in 2001. That is why you need to watch the charts in a manner that lets you make continuous comparisons at past market turns.

Under the Stochastic Oscillator you will find a new window with additional information called volume. Volume is a tally of all the trades coming into a market. The orders will either establish a new trading position or close out an existing position. Volume is cumulated and a tally is created for the day. The chart is always one day behind, so many traders use tick volume, price changes by the smallest fluctuation as another means of trading activity that is collected in a more timely, real-time interval. Actual order volume can be added to your charts to create total volume for the week or month to mirror the activity across the bars that were used to build the chart. When you are reading volume, look for relative changes.

In Figure 4.4, a declining line is drawn over volume at the bottom right to help you see that fewer trades are being made as time goes on under this line. Another form of divergence occurs when the market is advancing but fewer people are participating. This divergence in volume is viewed as confirmation of the divergence warning between price and the oscillator.

Note in Figure 4.4 how the volume has a few bars that are extremely high. They occur at exact pivot areas. Volume that suddenly runs to an extreme near the end of a lengthy trend is called *capitulation*. This situation is a panic and draws in the last of the sellers (in this case as they panic to dump their shares). After such a panic, who is left to sell? No one. Thus, to a smart trader capitulation provides valuable information that a *washout* panic can present an opportunity. If the washout forces the market down to a major price support zone, it can become a significant buy signal because that low should not be challenged again if the market is reversing.

Figure 4.5 is a weekly chart for Microsoft (MSFT). In this chart prices are making new lows when the oscillator is making higher lows in 2000 and 2002. The bullish divergence indicates that the selling pressure is dwindling, and in

Technical Analysis Demystified

Figure 4.4   Divergence Analysis in Veritas (VRTS)

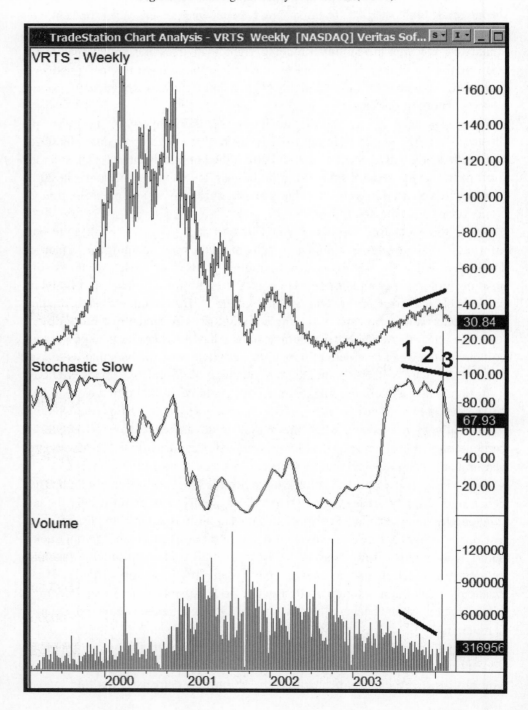

Figure 4.5   Weekly Chart for Microsoft (MSFT)

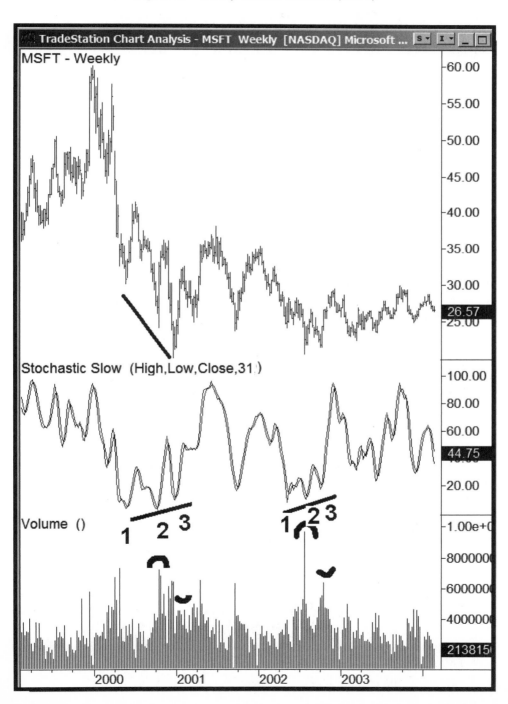

each case there is confirmation from volume. Note that the third divergence is accompanied by lower volume each time. What gives the second divergence signal in 2002 a higher grade is the fact that it forms at a price level similar to the signal in 2000.

In the second set of divergence signals in 2002, did you notice that the low marked 3 is not a true divergence? The price low is higher than the price low that matches point 2 in the second set. Here you need to use your smarts. Point 2 is a single spike downward that forms a capitulation event. The volume is at an extreme high that is the highest-volume week within the entire time frame of the chart. The price spike downward at point 2 in 2002 simply put a few people through the wash-and-rinse cycle. The panic selloff would have been caused when people believed that the old price low in 2000 would not support the market.

Another important consideration is that if the second set of divergence signals formed with volume confirmation and repeated the first signal, shouldn't MSFT stock explode upward? Yes! When it did not move in this manner, that was a warning to step out of the trade and reevaluate it. When a market decides to ignore a strong signal, it is developing a potential failure. Smart traders do not hang around to see if that is the case. If the market is not meeting expectations for any reason, get out immediately.

The signal was valid because MSFT bounced merrily toward $30. However, your stop loss should have protected most of your gains, and the rest of the action provides a dismal excuse to buy it again.

Figure 4.6 is a weekly chart for Goodyear Tire and Rubber (GT). You will recall that Goodyear had a quality problem with its tires in 2000. The chart shows the staggering collapse. In 2002 the MACD oscillator is diverging with the price lows from 2000. Do you think this is a valid divergence signal? It fits the description, but the divergence is very wide. The line under the momentum lows is a trend line that is touched twice. If the trend line were touched a third time, the signal would be much stronger. This is a weak signal that should be passed by. The reality for this chart is that it continued to advance into 2006. Clearly, additional information is needed to build confidence when the divergence pattern is too wide.

There is another question to consider: How can you get an even stronger signal without changing the method used in these charts? The answer is to look for the same signal in more than one time frame. For example, if there is divergence in a weekly chart and the same setup in a daily chart, the signal is much stronger than it would be if it formed only in one time frame. When the NASDAQ crashed, the signals formed in quarterly, monthly, and weekly charts. That's pretty serious and rare. Short-horizon traders should try comparing daily charts with 60-minute charts and trade when the two agree at a target zone.

Figure 4.6   Weekly Chart for Goodyear Tire and Rubber (GT)

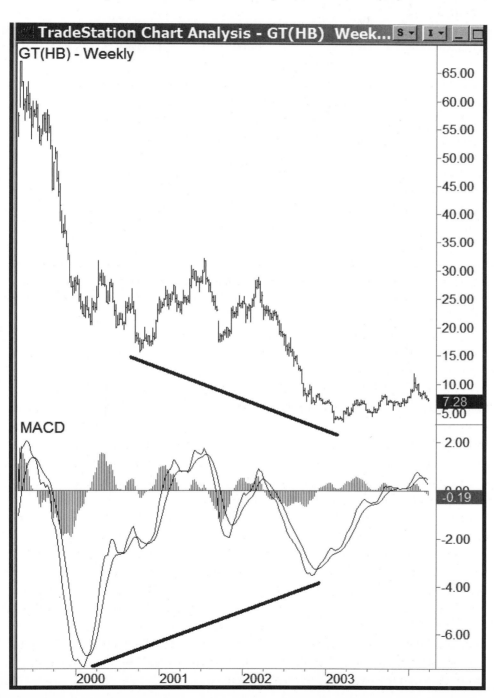

Quiz for Chapter 4

1. When a market is at an extreme overbought or oversold position, it can:
   a. No longer follow the price trend
   b. Be said that all participants are on the same side of the market
   c. Become even more overbought or oversold without making a correction
   d. No longer move in the same trend and must make an immediate price reversal to offset the excess sentiment

2. The long-horizon charts of the NASDAQ and Japanese Nikkei stock indexes both display which of the following?
   a. Market bubbles that implode and retrace the entire rally
   b. Mass public sentiment that runs to extremes, resulting in a sharp 50 percent correction
   c. Mass public sentiment that runs to extremes, showing that momentum indicators cannot be used
   d. Normal market swings within bull and bear market cycles

3. A weighted indicator is:
   a. An indicator that is given greater importance in a series of formulas used to develop a strategy
   b. An indicator manipulated to give greater significance to the strongest market swing
   c. An indicator back-adjusted so that market gaps do not influence results
   d. An indicator formula adjusted across the data series to give the more recent data more significance than the oldest data

4. A look-back period is:
   a. A set of fixed cycles showing similarities in market movement
   b. A defined period of time for study
   c. A critical point in historical data such as the Great Crash of 1929
   d. A defined historical price range regardless of the period for study

5. Whipsaw is a term used to describe which of the following?
   a. A specific pattern that will lead to continuation of the larger trend
   b. A trading style of rapid entries and exits by floor traders

    c. A market that keeps changing directions, stomping out all traders regardless of whether they are short or long

    d. A directional signal that forms a hook and traps traders in a gap in the opposite direction

6. When a short-period average is above a long-period average on price data:

    a. A positive spread develops because the faster average creates a positive spread with the slower average

    b. A negative spread develops as the longer-period average is subtracted from the shorter-period indicator

    c. A, and a sell signal forms in the indicator

    d. C, and a trader should enter an option straddle to capitalize on the positive spread developing in the market

7. Detrending is a method of:

    a. Drawing trend lines on the price data to form parallel channels

    b. Taking the spread difference of two averages and plotting the result as a displacement from zero

    c. Using trend lines so that they track back-adjusted data to define important angles for future trend analysis

    d. Taking the spread between averages and multiplying the result by the current closing price to define complex trends

8. A normalized indicator is:

    a. An indicator representing the normal price action of a particular market

    b. An indicator referencing a market in a specific year and with the price set as zero

    c. An indicator normalized by back-testing data over a very long historical reference period

    d. An indicator formula adjusted so that it cannot exceed 100 or fall below zero

9. When a line drawn over price highs diverges with a line drawn over the highs developing in the relative strength index, this is called:

    a. Bullish divergence

    b. Positive divergence

    c. Bearish divergence

    d. Negative divergence

10. When a line drawn to connect price lows converges with a line drawn to connect the momentum lows of any momentum oscillators, this is called:

a. Bearish divergence

b. Bullish divergence

c. Negative divergence

d. Positive divergence

CHAPTER 5

Does Price Data Give Clues about Direction?

Directional Signals

So far the discussion has demonstrated that technical analysis is closely connected with psychology. Because the price data encompass everything that market participants believe is true at any specific moment, the price data alone can tell the story. The weekly chart for Citigroup (C) in Figure 5.1 shows the first directional signal. Directional signals require immediate action because they paint a precise picture of what is brewing. In this way they are different from market patterns.

Figure 5.1 Weekly Chart for Citigroup (C)

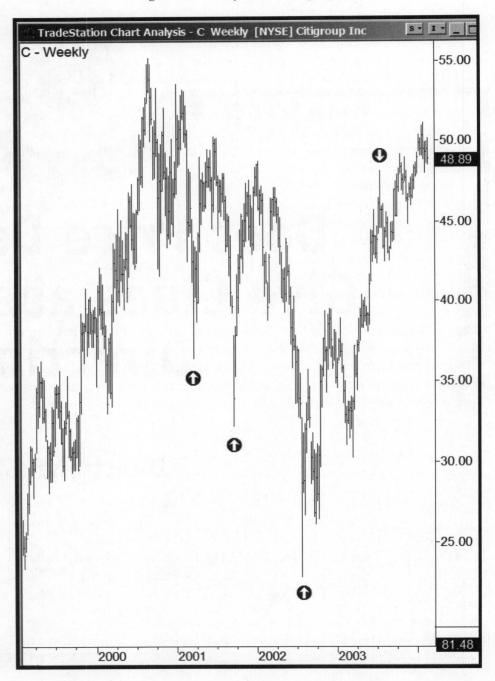

KEY REVERSALS

The Citigroup chart shown in Figure 5.1 has four arrows marking extreme declines that immediately end a market swing. These sharp declines are called *key reversals* and often are accompanied by volume that spikes, making them a *capitulation key reversal*. They define a market washout that occurs when a panic has flushed most of the market participants out of the positions they held when the spike moved sharply downward. When a key reversal forms into a market high, the sellers are forced to cover their positions by buying back the stock they sold short. Whether the spike is into a high or a low, the reversal often halts the market for a period, and smart traders who are not trapped in the panic can step aside before the runaway freight train speeds through.

The only people trying to buy the price lows are institutional traders who have ways to examine the risk exposure more precisely. You were introduced to one of these methods when we looked at using multiple Fibonacci ratios. But professional traders also have experience and ways to hedge their position. That move is not as gutsy when a trader has capital to spread across a few strategies and ways to protect against losses by holding positions on both sides of the market at the same time. This means you may be long and short in the same position, but the timing is different. There are complex strategies that minimize some of the risk, but their use requires very deep pockets. Is there a safer way to trade these sharp spikes? They do indicate that the trend will reverse rapidly, but smart traders avoid ulcers and wait. The market rips to the reverse and then makes an effort to retrace the spike bar. However, more patient traders will wait for the retracement and must be aware of a 61.8 percent retracement of that specific bar.

As the market pulls back, retracing a downward spike, the pullback should not break below the 61.8 percent retracement. This indicates that the market has regained some strength, and the safer place to enter the new trend is during this retracement. Look at the actual low marked with a downward-pointing arrow at the far right in Figure 5.1. The deep retracement does not break $25, and it is clear that a strengthening momentum indictor will accompany this pullback. Therefore, price and momentum are on your side. The directional signal is immediate, but your trading strategy does not have to be as quick. The exception would be if you held a short position when the spike developed. If this happens, get out; take the profits and run.

I have met very few traders who can reverse their entire position by switching from being short to being long in the market in a single order. To do that, you have to enter an order twice the size of your original one so that you end up with a position that is working the opposite market direction with a position of the same size. Mentally, that is tough to do. I like to cover and have a brief setup time to ponder my next move. It might be only a 3-minute pause on the sidelines, but that pause helps me switch my thinking and plan my attack.

RAILWAY TRACKS

Figure 5.2 is a monthly chart for Ford (F). The chart shows three strong reversals that are marked with arrows. If the chart covered 2 months, which is something most vendors cannot produce, it would look just like Figure 5.1, which was used to demonstrate directional key reversals. These key reversals also are called *railway tracks*. The bars spike side by side and mark the death of a trend. Figure 5.2 provides a dramatic illustration of railway track directional signals. Every buyer who was enticed to buy within the rising spike was stepping into a trap. The market reversed so quickly that every buyer in the previous month would have been under water, that is, in a position that was losing money.

The market rarely gives you a gracious exit when this pattern forms. If you think about it, it traps short sellers as well. Remember the point I made about making a 61.8 percent retracement target of the key reversal bar? Here the market has produced what is called a *short squeeze* by panicking short sellers who were only a little bit early. If you had placed a stop loss order just over the high of the first bar, the market would have nailed you and then moved rapidly away in the direction in which you believed it would go. The way to handle such a sharp swing is always to manage your risk and be prepared to deal with a worst-case scenario. It goes without saying that it is critical to know how much or little money you should put in the market. You will learn more about risk assessment in Chapter 6.

CAUTION

You may find wild price spikes all through a daily stock chart. It is as if the character of the stock just wants to make this key reversal style swing tops and bottoms at every turn. This is a warning not to trade that stock symbol. Either the market is very thin, meaning that the volume traded in the stock is small, or the stock is an over-the-counter symbol and the market maker is running the stops to make extra income. This happens sometimes, and you need to pay attention to specific stock symbols if you see frequent key reversals in the daily intra-day data.

Figure 5.2   Monthly Chart for Ford (F)

REVERSAL DAY

The third directional signal is shown in Figure 5.3. (The name of the stock in this daily chart is of little importance because you will find this directional signal in any market. You need to become aware of the size of a bar as it relates to its neighbors.) Does the bar engulf its earlier neighbors and then close well above the range of the bar beside it? Does the bar that follows this action show continued strength and then close above the highs of the preceding day? In Figure 5.3 you'll recognize a spike in volume. This is called *capitulation*. However, the juxtaposition of the three boldface bars creates a specific directional signal that is called a *reversal day*. If you did not act on the capitulation, you would have reacted on the second day as the stock rose above the highs of the bar marked with an arrow. The reason for this is demonstrated clearly in the daily bar that follows the bars in boldface: The market lifts like a rocket.

BEARISH SIGNALS

The data in Figure 5.4 show another directional signal. This chart uses only two bars to create the signal. When the market makes a new high and the next day fails to extend the gain and closes below the lowest traded price of the day before, you know that the market has run out of juice. This is a *bearish signal*. It does not indicate just how bearish and overextended the market is currently and how far a decline will develop, but it warns you that a correction is near.

Figure 5.5 shows a low in Johnson & Johnson (JNJ). The signal is made up of two bars, but the figure shows that they do not have to be side by side. Here the closing price for the day is above the high of a low day. This juxtaposing of price bars can signal that a trend reversal has just begun. In this chart it shows that the timing of the signal and the actual market turn was excellent.

ISLAND REVERSAL

Figure 5.6 shows a daily candlestick chart that clearly displays another type of directional signal: an *island reversal*. This signal is tricky, as the market produces a price gap between the range of the last day and the present range. The market makes a bold effort to stay above the gap it produced, but that effort ends in failure. The market opens a session by moving back down through the gap it formed on the chart. This is a serious failure when it develops in stocks. In this example, the Japanese yen futures fail to trade between .7691 and .7756. That is a big gap. The chart pattern is an island reversal, but the trader needs to look further to extract more detail from other methods such as volume or supporting oscillators.

Candlesticks

You can use a chart style to emphasize the range traded relative to the opening and closing prices. Small rectangular boxes are drawn to denote the range of the spread between the opening and closing prices. The session may make price lows or highs beyond the rectangles. These extra ranges are referred to as the wicks of a candlestick. They look a little like candles, and they have been adopted from the Japanese, who prefer them to bar charts. Although the Japanese look for specific patterns that form in candle groups or in single candles, you can use these charts to help you create support and resistance targets. View a few candlestick charts on the Internet or use a computer to create your own. You can draw horizontal lines to connect the real bodies of the candles. The real bodies are the rectangles that connect the open and close.

FOREX

We have been looking at stock data, but other markets form gaps as well with different reasons why they can occur. Currencies trade 24 hours a day because foreign exchange (FOREX) is always on the move somewhere in the world. Currency futures are traded in Chicago only during the daytime hours, but they can trade overnight in a night session outside of Chicago. Is this an island reversal or a gap to show a closed market or trading session? Novice traders make far too many assumptions about charts associated with futures markets. I recommend that you stay with American stocks when you are learning and not touch futures until you understand the risks involved. Futures have far greater risk because of the extreme leverage they allow. You have to pay out about 4 percent of the real value of a futures contract. That means the dollar loss for a minor move can be exponentially greater than it is in a stock position.

Futures also experience something called *locked limits*. This means that you can have a position that moves against you, and the market suddenly decides to close any time within the daily session. You become trapped and cannot enter an order to escape a losing trade because the exchange is not open for business. This condition can go on for days, and when the market finally begins to trade, you have to sell your home to pay back the loss to the futures exchange. If you are trading currency future markets, you need to know something called "exchange for physical" and a host of other new variables because futures are tied to the spot, or cash market. Keep it simple in the beginning, and as tempting as it may be, do not trade futures until you have learned about the risk.

Figure 5.3 Market Directional Signal: Reversal Day

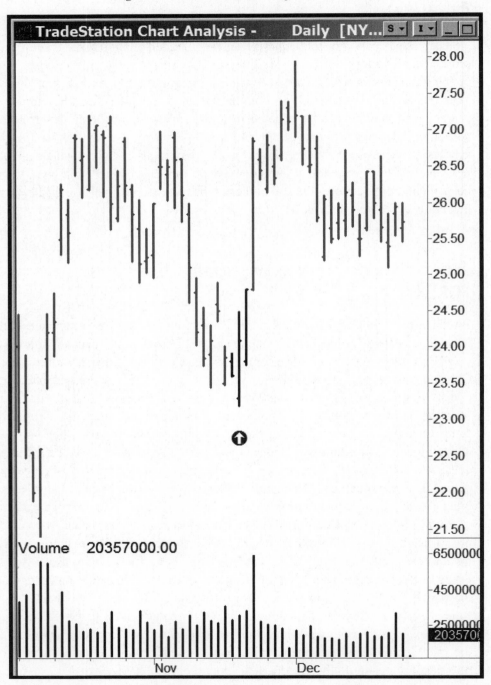

Figure 5.4 A Bearish Directional Signal

Technical Analysis Demystified

Figure 5.5 A Bullish Directional Signal; Daily Chart for Johnson & Johnson (JNJ)

Figure 5.6   An Island Reversal in Japanese Yen Futures

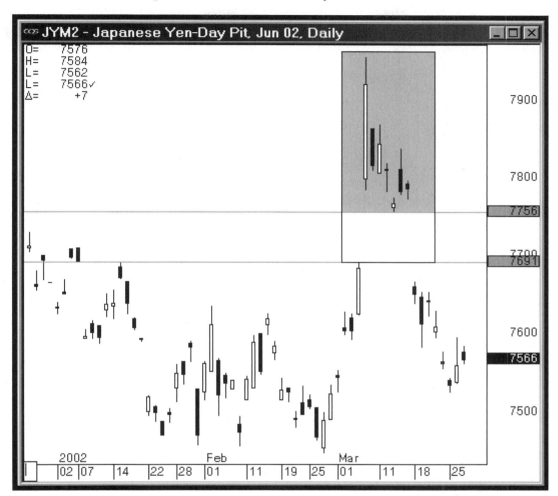

GAPS

Figure 5.7 shows a price gap when no trading has occurred. These gaps do occur in stocks and can have specific meanings. When a gap develops near the reversal of an old trend with increasing volume, that gap often develops after there is news about the stock. The increased volume is the key, and this is called a *breakaway gap* because the price gap often is not filled. As the trend becomes more mature, the majority of traders may find themselves on the same side of the market. This becomes a point of recognition that is good for some and ugly for others. If you are

Figure 5.7   Gaps, Breakaway, Runaway, and Exhaustion

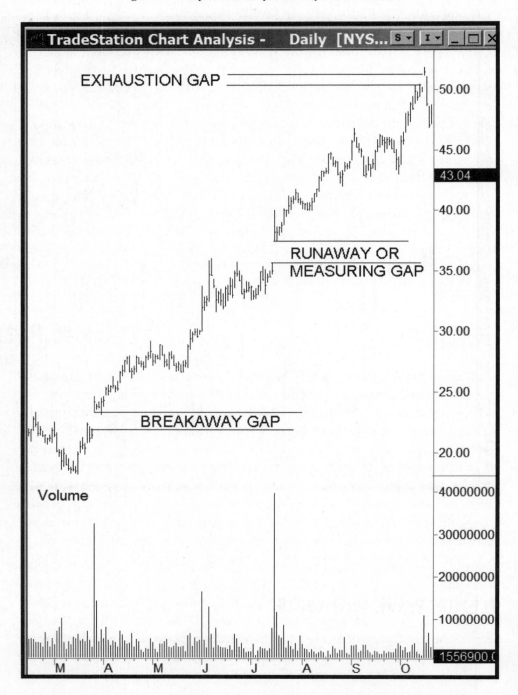

on the wrong side of the market at this juncture, the only thing you can do is cover the losing trade. The traders on the right side are buying more because they know that a *runaway gap* can be used to measure a new target equal to the range under the gap. Everyone is scrambling on the same side of the market for one reason or another at this point. This causes the stock to open higher than it did in the preceding session, thereby forming the gap in traded prices. This also is called a *measuring gap* because it often marks the midpoint of the move.

In Figure 5.7, the difference between the price low near $18 and the middle of the gap near $36 is $18. By adding this difference of $18 to the $36, you get a price target of $54. You can see that this stock made a strong effort to reach that target. Near the end of a trend, a stock may encounter a late gap that does not follow through on the next day. This immediate slip down through the gap is a directional signal that indicates that the market is exhausted. As a result, these gaps are called *exhaustion gaps*. They often start corrections. The same gaps develop in downtrends. Here, a rally is being used to examine the different types of gaps found in the price data.

Market Patterns

As the name implies, a *continuation pattern* is a consolidation that allows the nearby excesses to work themselves out of the market. Then the larger trend resumes.

The daily chart for JC Penney (JCP) in Figure 5.8 forms a continuation pattern. A consolidation forms against the larger downtrend, and the outer dimension of the correction forms a flag pattern. This is called a *bearish flag* that warns traders that the resumption of the downtrend will occur when the corrective flag is complete. I am not an advocate of using these patterns, but everyone knows what they look like, and so should you since they are a beacon for flagging mass psychology within a group of traders. The problem with continuation patterns is the risk they bear as a trading signal. You rarely know when the pattern is over, and so it draws you in early. Use them for analytic purposes only and you will be better off.

ELLIOTT WAVE PRINCIPLE

The bearish flag discussed in Figure 5.8 is also known as an *Elliott Wave Principle* pattern. The pattern has three swings, and the first and last swings are nearly the same length. If you knew that corrective patterns needed three swings to be complete

Figure 5.8   Daily Chart for JC Penney (JCP) Showing a Continuation Pattern

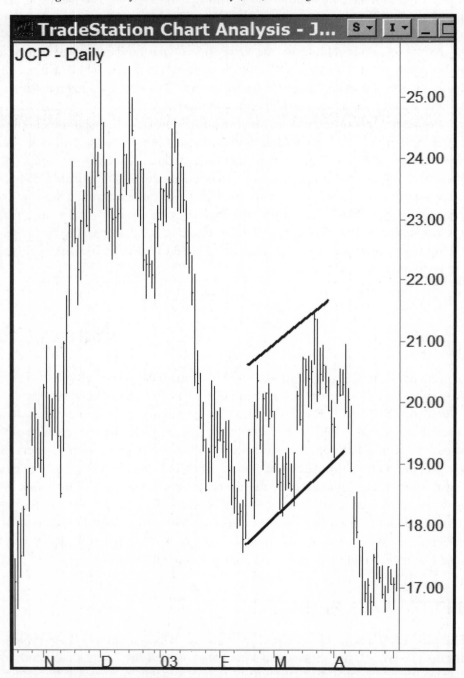

and used the Fibonacci technique to determine a price target, you would be in a stronger trading position than that of a trader using the bearish flag pattern alone.

It is becoming increasingly important to be aware of what is happening overseas. Figure 5.9 shows a monthly chart for the Japanese government 10-year bond. Why

Figure 5.9   Monthly Chart for Japanese Government 10-Year Bond (JGB)

should you be interested in this market? The Japanese 10-year bond market has been leading all the other global bond markets for several years. This is like buying tomorrow's data so that you can examine it today ahead of the market opening in U.S. government 10-year bonds. (If you would like to know more about how markets can indicate where another market is heading before that event occurs, refer to my book *All About Technical Analysis*. It is important to be aware of global markets and to develop charting techniques that help you make comparisons. Those techniques are spelled out in that book.)

In this chart, the Japanese government bond (JGB) was in a rally from 1994 to 2003. There are two consolidations marked in the chart that look like triangles on their sides. These triangles are called *bullish pennants*. (Some people call these patterns *bullish contracting triangles*. Both names imply that a market is making a sideways correction that is coiling in ever-tightening swing ranges.) When the pattern is complete, the move is strong and forms a thrust in the direction in which the market was going before the interruption. For this reason everyone takes note of this coiling market action, but most step in too early, get chopped badly, and have to stay out by the time the real move begins. The best way to trade these patterns is to be very patient and establish your position on a breakout of the pattern.

When the market breaks through the upper trend line of the pattern, it often makes a test of the same trend. That is the point at which to enter a trade because you know that the market should not reenter the consolidation. Therefore, you can make a judgment not to hold your position if the market moves only a small amount against you. Another time to trade these patterns is when the lower boundary is broken. The market moving out of a bullish triangle on its lower side is a failure. Failures are directional signals that should be acted on quickly.

A market that has been declining in its larger trend and forms one of these consolidations is called a *bearish pennant* or *bearish contracting triangle*. The outcome is the same, though in reverse. The pattern occurs in all markets and time horizons.

The weekly Microsoft (MSFT) chart in Figure 5.10 shows another bullish pennant or contracting triangle. This particular consolidation helps describe the internal character of these consolidations. They always have five internal swings. Each swing will have three smaller swings. The coiling pattern has been marked in this chart. The swings trade in a narrowing range so that lower highs and higher lows create the coiling action. Often the third, or middle, leg is tricky because it often takes the most time. That is not the case in this chart because this is the last consolidation before MSFT exploded upward into its final historical high.

The Dow Jones Industrial Average is a market that made a rather well-defined expanding triangle in 1996. That consolidation is shown in Figure 5.11. There are

Figure 5.10   Weekly Chart for Microsoft Showing a Contracting Triangle

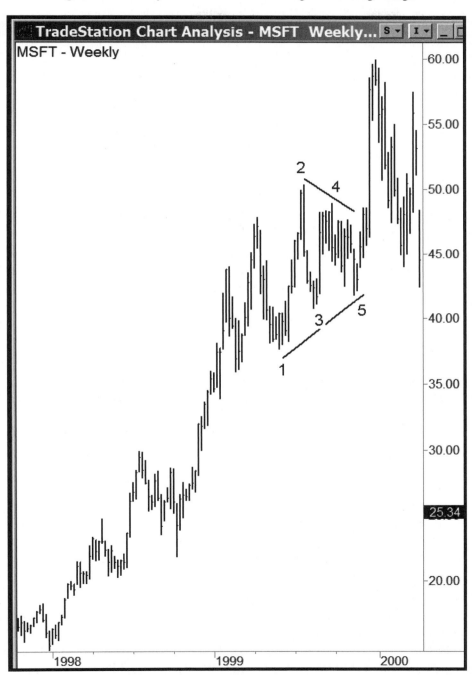

Figure 5.11 Expanding Triangle in the Dow Jones Industrial Average

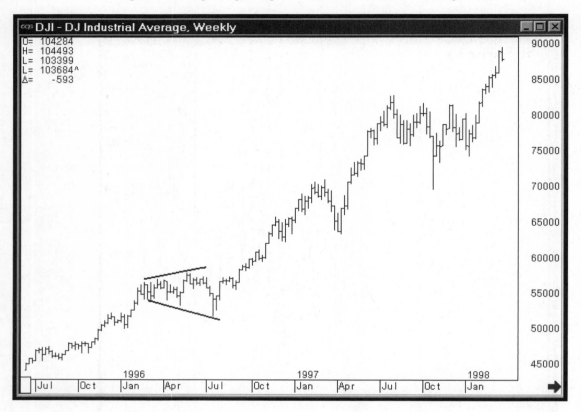

five swings, but can you find them? The first two are within the price chop defining the early stages of the correction. The market wastes no time making further gains when the continuation pattern is complete.

Review of Signals

Question: Figure 5.12 shows a directional signal in a monthly chart for Eastman Kodak (EK). The pattern is called a *diamond*, and it contains two triangles back to back. What makes this pattern a directional signal? You will have to examine the volume highlighted in a box under the pattern.

Answer: The second consolidation develops with declining volume. This warns you that the market is running out of steam before a major decline.

Figure 5.12   Diamond Directional Signal in a Monthly Chart for Eastman Kodak (EK)

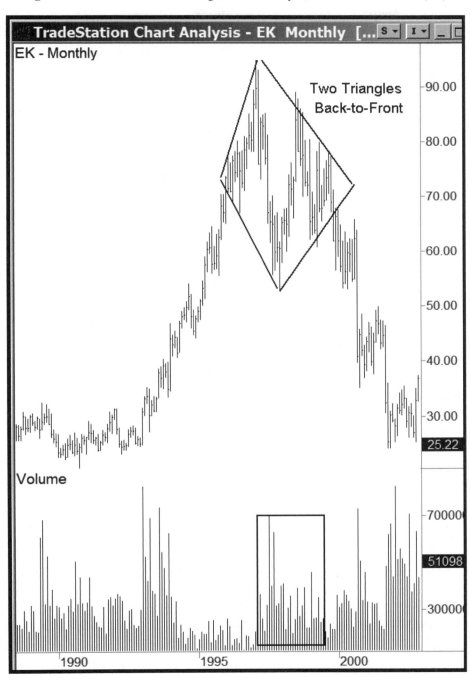

Question: A weekly chart for Amazon (AMZN) is shown in Figure 5.13. The chart shows that the stock made a key reversal into the first high in 1999. After a sharp decline, the market makes another effort to break out into a new high but fails and creates a second key reversal. Can you come up with a name for this particular chart pattern that warns that a major reversal could develop?

Answer: The actual pattern is called a *double top*. One also sees double bottoms or triple tops and bottoms. Do not forget what this chart looks like because it clearly shows a trend change. You could call it a reversal pattern or a directional signal because the outcome is always a trend reversal for a period. However, it does not necessarily mean that a total meltdown will follow, as can be seen with the Amazon stock.

Question: Figures 5.14 and 5.15 show two different reversal patterns. One shows a *rounded bottom reversal*, and the other shows a *reversal v-bottom*. I have not included the volume under these reversal patterns. What do you think the volume would look like in these two very different market reversals?

Answer: In the *reversal rounded bottom* the volume probably would be declining, as the number of orders to sell would be losing interest. The volume remains low because few people would be convinced that it was time to buy. Therefore, rounded bottom patterns have low volume that helps signal that a trend change is approaching. In the pattern called a reversal v-bottom, a spike in volume that is forming capitulation may accompany the price low. However, the low does not necessarily have to be so extreme. Perhaps the v-bottom is just showing increasing volume as people give up. The reversal and retracement of the decline warn that the trend may have reversed.

Question: Figure 5.16 shows a daily bar chart for AT&T. The second highlighted bar is called an *inside day* and can be viewed as a directional signal. Why is it called an inside day?

Answer: This is an inside day because the entire range of the trading session is less than the range defined by the opening and closing prices of the previous trading day. When a market cannot decide to buy or sell, it usually backs away to regroup for a period. This will help train your eye to look at small details within the relationships of your opening and closing prices.

Figure 5.13   Weekly Chart for Amazon (AMZN)

Figure 5.14 Rounded Bottom Reversal Pattern

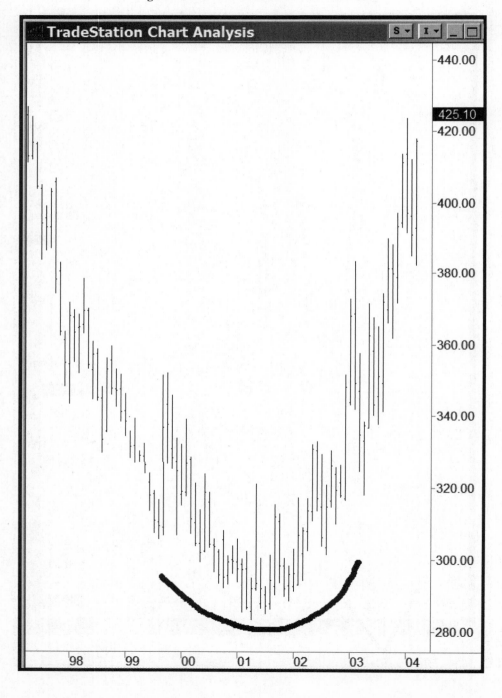

Figure 5.15 Reversal V-Bottom Pattern

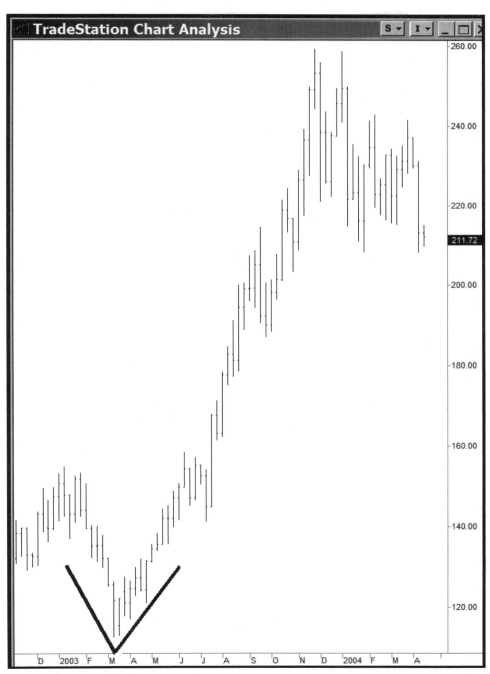

Figure 5.16   Daily Bar Chart for AT&T

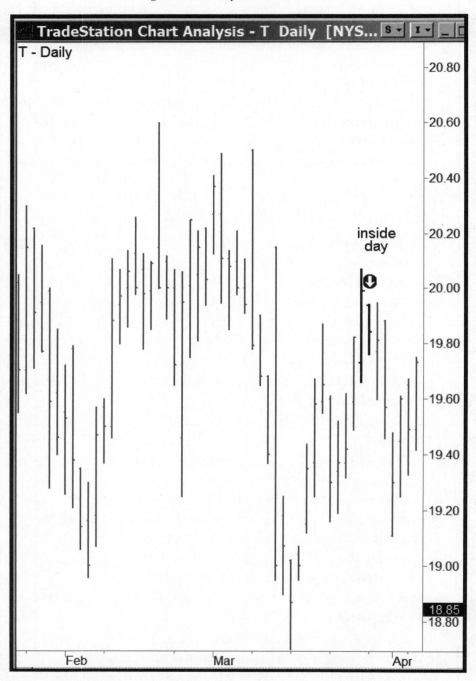

Quiz for Chapter 5

1. Directional signals tell a trader to:
   a. Add to an existing position as the direction is confirmed, requiring immediate action
   b. Take some or all profits immediately because the direction will reverse
   c. Be patient because a consolidation pattern is about to develop that will lead to further movement in the direction of the larger trend
   d. Be patient and wait for confirmation to enter the market when volume declines

2. A Key reversal is a:
   a. Continuation pattern
   b. Continuation signal
   c. Directional signal
   d. Directional pattern

3. Reversing a position means that a trader will do which of the following?
   a. Enter an order double the size of the original position in the opposite direction, becoming weighted equally in reverse of the prior open order
   b. Change his or her mind and exit the market
   c. Enter an order to go flat and then decide to enter an order of any size on the opposite side
   d. Look at a data chart flipped on the screen to remove any biases he or she may have

4. A stock chart displays numerous wild spikes at the lows and highs of most swings. You should view this market as:
   a. A market giving clear directional signals for swing traders
   b. A market with fundamental news about to be announced, with the gamblers taking positions ahead of the release
   c. One with very high institutional activity at the pivot levels, though it is hard to tell if they are adding to existing positions
   d. One with a market maker running the market at key pivots to his or her own benefit that is better left alone

5. The over-the-counter market is located in:
   a. A separate room in the New York Stock Exchange
   b. Any location where the market maker decides to set up his or her terminal

    c. A separate room in Chicago's Board of Trade

    d. A subdivision of the NASDAQ for smaller stocks

6. Capitulation is:

    a. A volume spike when the masses panic and exhaust a trending market

    b. The total number of outstanding shares of a stock symbol being traded

    c. The total number of shares divided by the volume over the same time interval

    d. An extreme spike in prices

7. A candlestick displays the:

    a. Open as a small tick mark to the left of a bar displaying the period price range

    b. Closing price as a black rectangular range

    c. Entire day's range within rectangles so that the ranges can be compared with one another more easily

    d. Open as the top of the real body

8. A gap develops in a mature trend. The gap is a warning if:

    a. It is accompanied by bearish divergence

    b. It is accompanied by higher volume

    c. It is accompanied by lower volume

    d. It is accompanied by a news report that has a temporary impact on the market

9. A market in which everyone is on the same side often forms:

    a. A runaway gap

    b. A key reversal

    c. An engulfing pattern in a candlestick chart

    d. A mass panic

10. A diamond is which of the following?

    a. A cutting remark about a novice trader

    b. Two back-to-back triangles in a price chart

    c. An option position that requires two long positions framing a single weighted short position

    d. A futures market in Russia

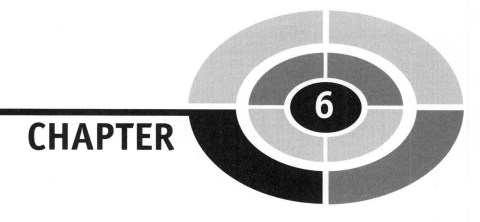

CHAPTER 6

How Do You Know When Something Will Happen?

Cycles

As mentioned in Chapter 1, economics professors have reported on business cycles for a couple of centuries. Human nature causes the same cycles to be repeated, but with a different twist each time. The markets are affected by mass psychology, and as a result cycles form that can help traders anticipate when something will happen.

Figure 6.1 shows a monthly chart for Goodyear Tire and Rubber (GT). At the bottom of the chart is the momentum indicator that was discussed in Chapter 4

Figure 6.1 Monthly Chart for Goodyear Tire and Rubber

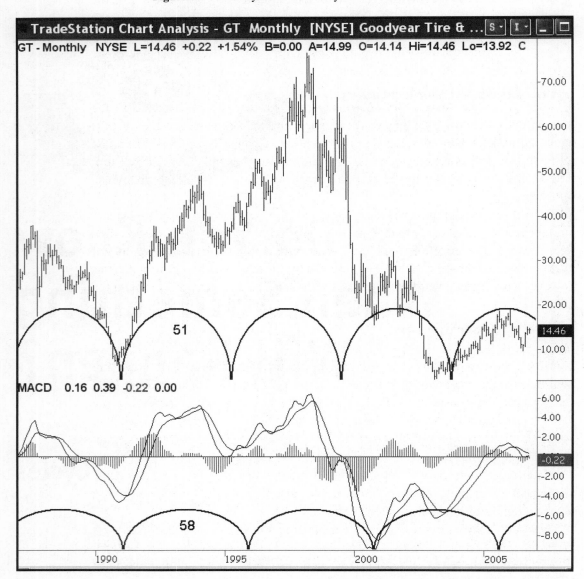

called MACD or moving-average convergence divergence. I have included this indicator here in Figure 6.1 to make a point. At the bottom of the price data in the middle of the chart you will see a series of arcs. The number 51 shows that I decided to place the spread of the arcs 51 months apart. (It was not rocket science; I just dropped the default tool and dragged one of the bottom lows until my eye told me it was a good fit.) The 51-period cycle fits fairly well since you want to match declines and their bottoms to the lows of the arcs. Let the highs go as they will. This suggests that a market low will develop at some point in 2003, but the cycle is late and the market bottoms before the cycle occurs.

That is going to happen often when only a single cycle is defined. A 58-period cycle (a period in this case means one bar, or a month) can be added to the momentum indicator. Oscillators in fact help you take advantage of the cyclical nature of markets. However, the big difference here is that a cycle that is placed on the indicator will not be a price low because momentum indicators do not turn with markets. If you trade too early, this method will slow you down to give you a safer entry.

There is one small problem with this method: A fixed-period cycle assumes that markets move in a linear fashion and never expand or contract the cycles as time goes forward. The price low in GT at the far right of Figure 6.1 is an example of how the market bottomed before the cycle and the cycle contracted. Your indicator, however, gave you no warning of this. How do analysts deal with this problem?

FIXED-TIME CYCLES

Figure 6.2 shows a monthly chart for General Electric (GE). On the far left there are two cycles in the chart which are anchored at the 1987 price low. The October 1987 crash used to be considered a fairly significant event. It is not considered a big move in the larger picture now, but it still makes a good starting point to add two cycles to the chart with different periods. One is very long, and the other is about two and a half times faster. These two cycles come together at a price bottom near the lows of the sharp decline. You should look for these cycles to agree and come into phase, or display confluence timing, because they tend to warn you that a higher-probability low will develop.

These two charts represent the conventional applications of cycles. However, the problem with fixed cycles is the natural tendency of prices to expand or contract. When markets are in strong rallies, they may expand by extending the length of their price swings before interim corrections occur. In a market that is contracting, you'll hit the price targets sooner and they will be lower than you expected. This is true with market timing: A fixed-time cycle will work sometimes, but at other times it will be late or early.

Figure 6.3 illustrates another tool used to find cycles. I recommend that you not use it to time trades. This is an analytic tool only. There is a big difference between

Figure 6.2 Monthly Chart for General Electric (GE)

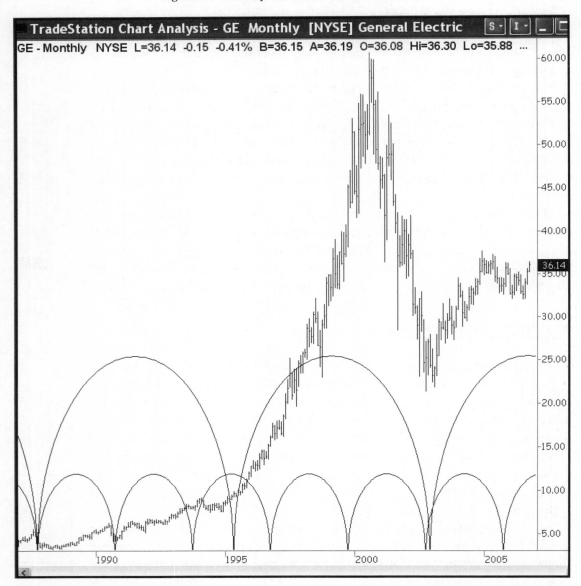

techniques used for analysis and techniques used for timing trades. Trading tools need to be precise when you are executing a trade. Analytic tools help you see approaching icebergs but generally cannot tell you when an iceberg will hit. Your studies undoubtedly will uncover methods that use advance-decline lines. These

Figure 6.3   Monthly Chart for General Electric Showing a Fibonacci Cycle in Time

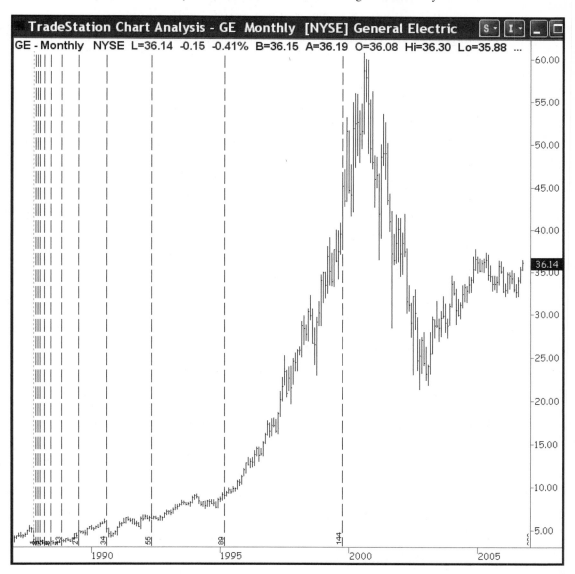

methods compare stocks advancing with stocks declining. The methods also include other comparisons, such as buying activity versus selling activity. In my opinion they have little value for a trader because it may take months before the imbalance begins to be seen in a market move; by that time your capital could be gone. This

belief has been viewed as heresy by some analysts, so make your own judgment when you read about these tools in other people's work.

Figure 6.3 is a monthly chart for General Electric (GE) with vertical lines. The lines originate from the 1987 low, and each line is drawn in conjunction with the growth cycle discussed in Chapter 3. A Fibonacci time cycle uses the periods 0, 1, 1, 2, 3, 5, 8, 13, 21, 34, 55, 89, 144, and so forth. Everything in the universe that has a growth or decay cycle will abide by this mathematical number series. Figure 6.3 shows a Fibonacci cycle in time. You can see that it is early to the market highs. When you trade, you need technical evidence to warn you that something is going to happen very soon. This chart shows that the cycle tool was accurate—the rally was developing a problem—but its timing in terms of the exact month the market topped was considerably off. Granted, the market was in what is called a *blow-off rally,* when sentiment can push prices to extremes. Fibonacci cycles frequently have this problem in a real-time scenario. Fixed-interval cycles and Fibonacci cycles are the two methods used most commonly today. You can get very fancy with them, but they are not great trading tools.

Cycle Analysis Using Natural Laws

The bullets above the price bars in Figure 6.4 are dates. They do not denote market highs or lows; they are just dates of significance within a specific month. The bullets mark dates only and could be applied to any chart in which the *x*-axis is used to plot weeks. Take a look at the intervals between the bullets. They do not occur at fixed period intervals. They are also impressive in their ability to indicate when a change in a market trend may occur. This is astronomy, not astrology. There is no interpretation of or meaning to the dates; they simply represent the math behind a cycle. In this case, every time the planet Mars shifted 30 degrees along its orbital path, a bullet was mapped on the chart. This is called an *ingress time study*. It is a purely mathematical relationship that is being plotted, and it is statistically viable over very large databases.

Because planets move in elliptical orbits, the cycle does not have a fixed-period interval. That is why the timing of the bullets displayed have irregular spacing. However, this is a cycle that has a correlation with market turns. Climatology has something to do with universal cycles, and agricultural crops depend on this cycle for the amount of rain, temperature, and sun exposure they receive. The economic cycle is affected strongly by the cost of food. Did you know that sunspots that

Figure 6.4   Weekly Bar Chart for Amazon

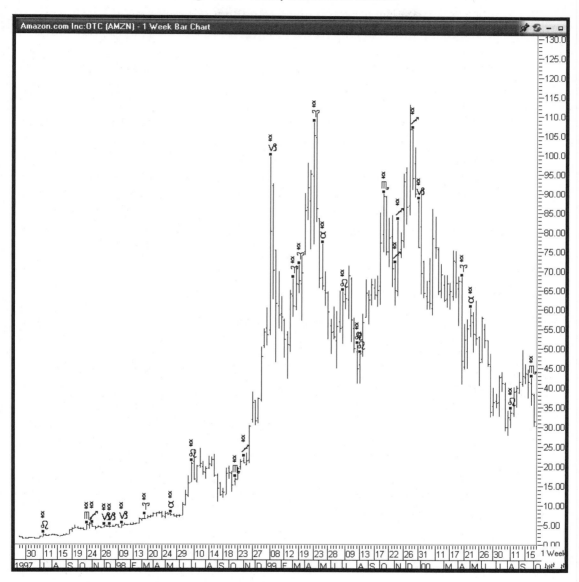

produce high solar flare activity increase the number of magnetic storms experienced on the earth? It has been proven that when there is high solar flare activity, there are higher crop yields. The result is lower prices in agricultural futures markets.

Sunspots trigger solor flares or storms. Sunspots are evidenced by dark spots on the sun. They occur when the lines of the sun's magnetic field become twisted. There are more sunspots when the sun is more active. This activity produces more radiation that can affect the earth's ionosphere. The sunspot cycle lasts approximately 22 years. It too is not a fixed cycle, but it does have an extremely high correlation to the prices of commodities. During times of high solar activity, there is more radiation from the sun, and the resulting higher ionization levels in the F-layer allow higher frequencies to be reflected. For example, around the solar maximum, the 10-meter band (28 to 30 MHz) is frequently open for extended periods, and long distances can be worked with rather low power levels.

During these high-activity periods, there are high yields of agricultural crops and hence low prices. In times of little or no activity, seasons of draught produce low crop yields and higher prices. The first decade of the twentifirst century is one of very high sunspot activity, and agricultural products are trading at extremely low prices.

John H. Nelson and the American Institute of Electrical Engineers

One of the things that helped me become comfortable with using astronomy in my trading was my discovery of the work of John H. Nelson, a radio propagation analyst for RCA. The way sound waves bounce back to earth under cloud cover is called propagation. In 1952 Nelson delivered a paper to the American Institute of Electrical Engineers titled "Sunspots and Planetary Effects on Short Wave Radio." He found that favorable and unfavorable radio transmission is associated with key planetary aspects or angles between the positions of planets. What astounded Nelson's colleagues in 1952 was his prediction of a magnetic storm some time near August 1959 that might cause a blackout of radio transmission over the North Atlantic. The Consolidated Edison Company of New York recorded a major power outage August 17, 1959.

On November 9, 1967, approximately 80,000 square miles of the Northeast fell into darkness. The impact was felt across eight states. Photographs show a Quebec-Hydro plant being damaged by an X-flare magnetic storm after a solar event. You will not find the technical explanation in the newspapers, but it appears in corporate reports for the major conductor lines. The effect was felt first in Toronto, Canada, where it reportedly went dark at 5:15 p.m. Rochester followed at 5:18 p.m. and then

Boston at 5:21 p.m. New York lost power at 5:28 p.m. The failure affected 4 million homes in the New York metropolitan area and left between 600,000 and 800,000 people stranded in the subway system.

The point that struck me about the blackout was the fact that measurable changes in magnetic fields around the earth can and do affect climatology, propagation radio signals, and probably a whole host of stuff I did not explore once I got the idea. I can accept changes in magnetic fields as a potential trigger for cycles because the charts are available and can be statistically evaluated. However, accepting magnetic storms as a cycle to monitor opens a Pandora's box of questions.

SOLAR ECLIPSES AND TRADING

Figure 6.5 is a monthly chart for Caterpillar (CAT). The small circles over the dark bullets mark the months that had a solar eclipse. The point is that timing for market swings can be determined. You may not like the reasons behind the cycles, but the charts are hard to ignore when they work. The bullets in this chart actually fit a specific day within the months that are marked. I dropped these charts down to the shortest time frame to try to time market turns with my price targets and indicators. Demonstrating the point with a longer-horizon view is most useful for now.

What about lunar eclipses? They are more important in Asian markets, whereas the solar cycle is tracked more closely in North America. I do not know why, but back-testing to see if there is a correlation present gives repeatable results. Some stock sectors will be more attuned to one cycle than to another. An example is a housing stock called Centex Corporation (CTX), which is the subject of Figure 6.6.

Figure 6.6 (on page 113) shows an ingress study, but for a different planet. The funky-looking "*h*" is the glyph for Saturn. Every time Saturn moves to a precise 30-degree location in its progressive orbit, a mark is made on the chart. The cycle is not fixed. This is a study based on geocentric relationships that puts the earth rather than the sun at the center. Sometimes you will find a tight cluster of three bullets. This is due to a phenomenon called *retrograde*. If you consider the solar system mathematically by putting the earth in the middle, the elliptic paths of the planets become distorted as they are viewed from the earth.

Retrograde is like the idea of two speeding trains running in the same direction. As the faster train passes the slower train, there is a brief period when the slower train seems to be moving backward. It is the same idea with the orbital path that the planets track. The perception is that a planet briefly tracks backward (retrograde)

Technical Analysis Demystified

Figure 6.5   Monthly Chart for Caterpillar (CAT)

when viewed from the earth and then goes forward (direct) again. In some studies of time, retrograde creates a small cluster of bullets. Figure 6.8 will demonstrate a retrograde cycle in a chart, but first look at Figure 6.7, which adds another cycle to Centex to capture more of the pivot swings.

Figure 6.6   Two-Week Bar Chart for Centex Corporation (CTX)

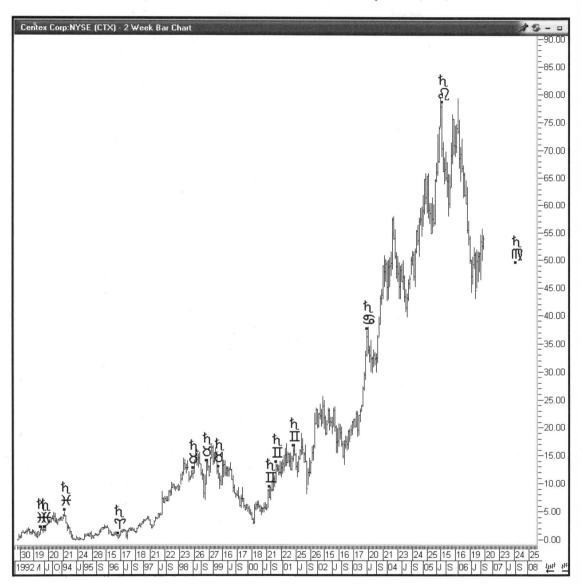

Figure 6.7 is a 2-week chart for Centrex that shows the same ingress study plotted in Figure 6.6. Note that a 2-week chart is much more revealing because it shows more accurately when a cycle has missed the actual market turn. If you find that the market is within plus or minus three bars, that is viewed as exceptional. This time I

Figure 6.7   Chart for Centrex with Multiple Cycles

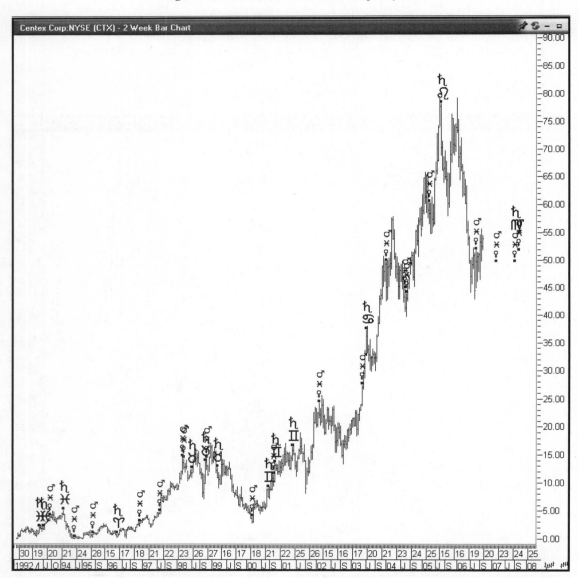

have added a mathematical angular relationship between two planets. Every time Mars and Venus have an exact 60-degree relationship with a separation of no more than 4 degrees, the date is marked on the chart. This is an example of an aspect cycle. The 60-degree relationship is called *sextile*. The angles you should study are

60, 90, 120, 180, and a full return, which is 360 degrees, or a conjunction when the separation is less than 4 degrees total.

Figure 6.8 shows a monthly chart for Caterpillar (CAT). You studied a solar eclipse cycle in the same chart in Figure 6.5. Figure 6.8 compares the two. Bullets

Figure 6.8   Monthly Chart for Caterpillar

mark the months in which Jupiter and Saturn progress 15 degrees. The glyph for Jupiter looks like the numeral 4. The glyph for Saturn is an "h" with a horizontal line in the first downstroke. Jupiter is closer to the earth, and so its cycle is faster and produces more notations in the chart. These cycles have the greatest impact when they occur together over a narrow time period. This is the same idea as confluence within price targets.

Figure 6.9 shows the same periods marked in Figure 6.8, but this study includes the sextile or 60-degree separation between Mars and Venus. There are two large brackets in this chart. The cluster that is fairly tight and narrow (the one on the left) marks a high that nearly leads a test back to the lows in 2002.

The bracket in 2004 marks another signal that no other technical method or cycle study can offer. It is a warning not to trade a market. This is the reason I use these methods. It is one thing to have a great trade in a super trending market, but you will find that it often is accompanied by a period when you give money back because there is nothing to extract from the market's chop. In Figure 6.9 the wide congestion of numerous bullets from these different cycles is a warning to stay away until the bullets are behind you on the calendar. As you can see in this chart, CAT was in a corrective chop for most of 2004.

That is one of the strengths of using astronomical periods. It is as valuable to know when to step into a trade as it is to know when to stay out of a market. One last comment: Ignore your momentum signals when these periods of congested cycles form in a single chart. It is not a problem when you use two charts to time a momentum signal because most likely they will be in disagreement and will not give you a signal to step into the market.

The chart in Figure 6.10 applies the concepts discussed in Figures 3.2 and 3.3 to demonstrate how to subdivide a range into eighths to suggest support levels. However, in Figure 6.10 a Saturn retrograde cycle has been added. The key reversal low in 2001 was near one of the divisions into eighths. The directional signal is a railway track formation, and it coincides with the time cycle when Saturn returned to a direct orbital motion. The market high occurred when Saturn went into a retrograde period. When it returned to direct motion again as perceived from earth, the cycle was complete. This also defined the duration of the trend for that price data swing.

This topic of cycles is controversial, but helps to raise your awareness that markets may be influenced by cycles impacting our entire planet in ways we are still discovering.

The best known analyst for cycle analysis was Edward R. Dewey, who created the Foundation for the Study of Cycles. His work remains highly respected today

Figure 6.9   Monthly Chart for Caterpillar with Sextile Cycles

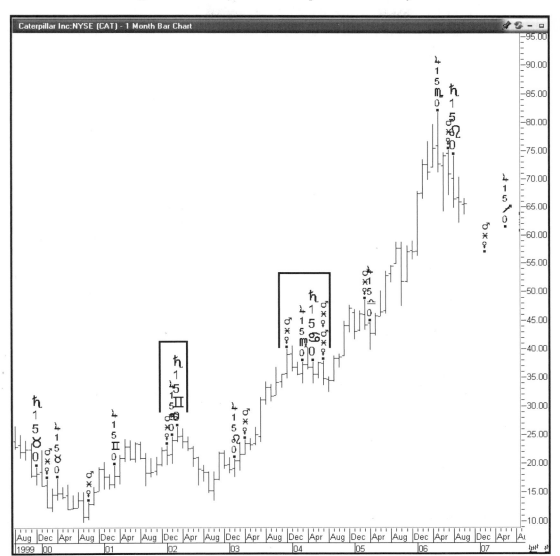

and is still studied closely by professionals. There is a book long out of print you should try to find called *Cycles: The Mysterious Forces That Trigger Events* by Edward R. Dewey, 1971, Hawthorn Books, Inc. In this book he included diagrams that show that nature has measurable cycles. He used a fixed interval to chart the average peaks. In this application it is highly useful as the cycle interval provides

Figure 6.10 Five-Week Chart for Adobe Systems with a Saturn Retrograde Cycle

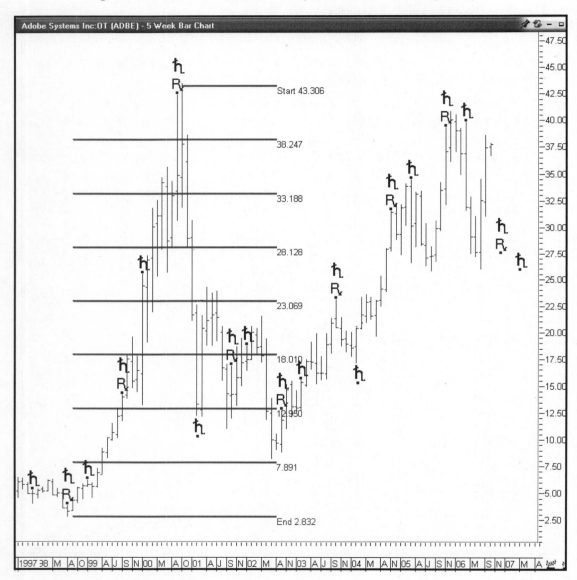

us with proof of there being cyclical changes, however an exact date implying something will happen is not given. Cycles show us fluctuations in trends.

Some of the diagrams in his book show extensive research in order to chart the rhythmical finding. There is a 9.6-year cycle in Lynx abundance from 1735 to 1969.

Timing Tools and Gann Analysis

What kind of analysis is this? It is your first introduction to the timing tools used in Gann analysis. If you wish to go into this area of study further or plot the same information on your charts, there are three ways to do it:

- Most astrology software packages let you create a simple table to list the eclipses, ingress dates, and aspects of interest discussed in this chapter. One charting product is Market-Analyst.
- A product called Solar Fire or Kepler also can provide those useful lists. The software is designed for astrology analysis, but you can use it for astronomy calculations.
- Use a book called *The American Ephemeris for the 21st Century: 2000 to 2050*; you only have to look up the information you need in a table.

Figure 6.11 Ephemeris for October 2006

LONGITUDE — OCTOBER 2006

Day	PLANETS ›	☿	♀	♂	♃	♄	♅	♆	♇
1 Su		28♎19.5	0♎43.5	14♎52.7	18♏ 30.0	21♌22.0	11♓ 45.4		24♐15.4
2 M		29 43.8	1 58.3	15 32.2	18 41.5	21 28.1	11R 44.3		24 16.2
3 Tu		1♏ 7.0	3 13.2	16 11.8	18 53.1	21 34.1	11 42.3		24 17.1
4 W		2 29.2	4 28.0	16 51.5	19 4.7	21 40.0	11 40.3		24 18.0
5 Th		3 50.2	5 42.9	17 31.1	19 16.4	21 45.9	11 38.3		24 18.9
6 F		5 10.1	6 57.8	18 10.8	19 28.2	21 51.7	11 36.3		24 19.9
7 Sa		6 28.7	8 12.7	18 50.6	19 40.0	21 57.5	11 34.4		24 20.9
8 Su		7 46.0	9 27.5	19 30.3	19 51.9	22 3.2	11 32.5		24 21.9
9 M		9 2.0	10 42.5	20 10.2	20 3.9	22 8.8	11 30.8		24 23.0
10 Tu		10 16.6	11 57.5	20 50.0	20 15.9	22 14.3	11 28.8		24 24.0
11 W		11 29.6	13 12.5	21 29.9	20 28.0	22 19.8	11 27.0		24 25.1
12 Th		12 41.0	14 27.5	22 9.9	20 40.1	22 25.2	11 25.2		24 26.3
13 F		13 50.7	15 42.5	22 49.8	20 52.3	22 30.6	11 23.5		24 27.5
14 Sa		14 58.4	16 57.5	23 29.9	21 4.5	22 35.8	11 21.8		24 28.7
15 Su			18 12.5	24 9.9	21 16.8	22 41.0	11 20.1		24 29.9
16 M			19 27.7	24 50.0	21 29.2	22 46.2	11 18.5		24 31.1
17 Tu			20 42.8	25 30.2	21 41.6	22 51.2	11 16.9		24 32.4
18 W			21 57.9	26 10.4	21 54.0	22 56.2	11 15.3		24 33.7
19 Th			23 13.0	26 50.6	22 6.5	23 1.1	11 13.8		24 35.1
20 F			24 28.1	27 30.9	22 19.1	23 5.9	11 12.3		24 36.4
21 Sa			25 43.3	28 11.2	22 31.7	23 10.6	11 10.9		24 37.8
22 Su			26 58.4	28 51.6	22 44.3	23 15.2	11 9.5		24 39.2
23 M			28 13.6	29 32.0	22 57.0	23 19.8	11 8.1		24 40.7
24 Tu			29 28.7	0♏12.4	23 9.7	23 24.3	11 6.8		24 42.1
25 W			0♏43.9	0 52.9	23 22.5	23 28.7	11 5.5		24 43.5
26 Th			1 59.1	1 33.4	23 35.3	23 33.0	11 4.3		24 45.1
27 F			3 14.3	2 14.0	23 48.1	23 37.2	11 3.1		24 46.7
28 Sa		25R 2.1	4 29.5	2 54.6	24 1.0	23 41.3	11 2.0		24 48.2
29 Su		25 4.5	5 44.7	3 35.2	24 13.9	23 45.3	11 0.9	17D 1.9	24 49.8
30 M		24 58.7	6 60.0	4 15.9	24 26.9	23 49.3	10 59.8	17 1.9	24 51.4
31 Tu		24 44.0	8 15.2	4 56.6	24 39.8	23 53.1	10 58.8	17 1.9	24 53.1

Planet Ingress Dy Hr Mn	
♀ ♎ 8 6:16	SEPTEMBER
♂ ♎ 8 4:18	
☿ ♎ 12 21:08	
☉ ♎ 23 4:04	
♀ ♎ 30 10:03	
☿ ♏ 2 4:38	OCTOBER
☉ ♏ 23 13:28	
♂ ♏ 23 16:39	
♀ ♏ 24 9:59	

Last Aspect Dy Hr Mn		› Ingress Dy Hr Mn
2 3:17	☿ □	♒ 2 3:25
3 20:15	♇ ⚹	♓ 4 5:34
5 20:34	♇ □	♈ 6 5:33
7 20:06	♇ △	♉ 8 5:05
9 17:09	♄ □	♊ 10 6:07
12 0:23	♇ ☍	♋ 12 10:22
14 6:28	♂ □	♌ 14 18:39
16 21:02	♂ ⚹	♍ 17 6:17
19 8:19	♇ □	♎ 19 19:20
22 5:59	♂ ☌	♏ 22 7:55
24 6:57	☿ ☌	♐ 24 18:54
26 18:03	♇ ☌	♑ 27 3:48
29 1:31	☿ ⚹	♒ 29 10:18
31 5:32	♇ ⚹	♓ 31 14:12

› Phases & Eclipses Dy Hr Mn	
SEPTEMBER	
7 18:43	○ 15♓00
22 11:46	● 28♍20
22 11:41:16	● A 7'09"
OCTOBER	
7 3:14	○ 13 ♈ 43
14 0:27	‹ 20 ♋ 31
22 5:15	● 28 ♎ 40
29 21:26	› 8 ♒ 19

ECLIPSE
Sept/22/2006

Figure 6.11 shows a portion of an ephemeris page that gives details for October 2006. The table supplies the exact dates for astrological events. The information includes direct and retrograde station dates and times. The tables list aspectarian details of the outer planets, Jupiter through Pluto. Details include angles of separation such as sextile or 60 degrees. (The symbol is an asterisk.) All the glyphs and symbols are included in the front matter of the book. The planet ingress times are listed along with lunar and solar eclipses. On this page there is an "A" beside a symbol that denotes a solar eclipse. It is recorded that an annular solar eclipse occurred on September 22, 2006. (If you are trading outside North America in other markets, be sure to use the Swiss ephemeris. This is the standard for most calculations and software products, but you will need to make adjustments for your time zone.)

There is a 9.6-year cycle in Atlantic Salmon abundance as recorded from 1880–1956. Dewey charted a repeating cycle in Mass Human Excitability since the time of 500 BC to AD 1922. This means recording the cycle of geopolitical upheavals to human expansion in productivity. He found there are nine cresting waves in each century. The cresting waves correlate with astrological cycles. He mapped human cycles such as an 18.2-year cycle in marriage rates in the United States from 1869 to 1951. He also discovered a cyclical pattern of 18.2 years for Immigration into the United States from 1824–1950.

Knowing that a 6.4-year rhythm occurs in Aluminum production since 1885 to 1962 helps us look at industrial cycles and think about the impact this may have in the future. In the United States we hear about the decline in real estate prices daily. But Dewey charts a 18.5-year cycle in Real Estate activity since 1795 until 1958. This current slump is right on schedule. From 1874 to 1947 there was a 6 year cycle in steel production. The current rally in steel is fueled by growth in China. But it is right on schedule with this historic cycle as well. Which comes first? The trigger or the cycle? It suggests larger forces are acting upon us all the time.

Agricultural cycles clearly correlate with the sunspot activity and resulting magnetic storms from the sun. Do magnetic flares influence our magnet fields around the earth and influence our weather patterns? Weather is the primary factor for agriculture cycles. Dewey shows a study of average annual sunspot activity from 1700 to 1968. The peaks are near 22 years. We know of the 10.5–11 year agricultural cycle between high yielding crop production and poor yields. Can people be influenced by this magnetic activity? It can most certainly be suggested that we are because there is a chartable 22.5-year cycle in international battles from 1415 to 1930. There is a half-cycle of 11 years identified from 1760 to 1947 in the

United States. It makes one have a little more of an open mind about what the possible influences are impacting our planet and markets.

There is a 41-month rhythm in stock prices in Dewey's book on page 122 to show a period from 1868 to 1945. The history of markets and their people is fascinating. John D. Rockefeller was hounded by people trying to uncover the secret to his market timing. What was his secret market timing weapon? He knew about the 40- to 42-month cycle in stocks and traded against it to his advantage.

Cycles have always been and will always be influences in the future. A student of the markets will become a student of cycles in an effort to obtain a sense of timing.

Quiz for Chapter 6

1. Markets develop mathematical ratios between bull and bear market swings that are similar to the growth and decay ratios found in nature.

   a. False

   b. True

2. Fixed-interval cycles can be too elementary to provide consistent market timing.

   a. False

   b. True

3. Magnetic storms from solar flares may explain some historical power outages.

   a. False

   b. True

4. John D. Rockefeller traded with a great interest in a 40- to 42-month cycle.

   a. False

   b. True

5. Retrograde is an astronomical condition that may be of interest to market traders.

   a. False

   b. True

6. A high-probability market turn date can be identified before the market reverses.
   a. False
   b. True

7. History shows that market bubbles develop because later generations forget the lessons of the past.
   a. False
   b. True

8. Studies show that weather patterns and agricultural crop yields are correlated with a 22-year sunspot activity cycle.
   a. False
   b. True

9. A Stochastics Indicator should have a period set to half the value of an identified fixed cycle within the price data.
   a. False
   b. True

10. When two or more cycles fall within a confluence area or tight time period, that probably will make the market exaggerate a correction.
    a. False
    b. True

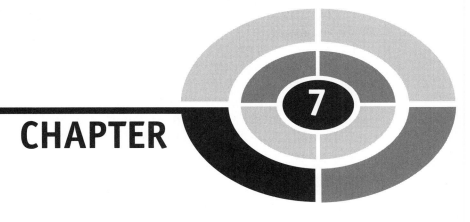

CHAPTER 7

Reasons to Enter the Market

This chapter is a little different from what you get in most books about trading: It is filled with market entry signals. I will show you which ones are most compelling and discuss others that are ho-hum but well-known. Learn them. Take notes on them. Then record in pictures and words your own signals that became triggers for action or the reasons you were motivated to take action and step into a position. Your notes will be valuable because they will show you why you made a good decision and why you might have missed something. Trading plays tricks with your mind. When you make a commitment and hold a position, your mind can convince you of anything, so take screen snapshots and write down why you made a trade entry not only to record what you need to change but also to reinforce what you did right.

The first thing you need to do is print a small sign that reads "Don't Move Until You See It" and tape it to the top of your computer screen. What is "it"? The phrase comes from the movie *Searching for Bobby Fischer.* "It" is the moment in the market when the methods you have been developing as your own tools come together to paint a clear picture. In other words, you should know exactly why you are doing what you're doing. That sign will save you a lot of money and give you the discipline to wait.

So what is it that you want to see? A series of events starting to come together on the screen will follow a specific logic tree. First you will use the price retracement technique that was covered in Chapter 3 using Fibonacci ratios to develop price projections. Then and only then, when you are on a price target, do you look for "permission" from your technical indicators. The entry signals that will be discussed next are signals that give you permission to take action. I will discuss where to enter the stops to manage your risk at the end of this chapter.

The first signal that it is time to get into a position is contained within a reversal pattern called a *head-and-shoulders pattern.* Figure 7.1 is a weekly chart for Amazon (AMZN) that shows the head-and-shoulders pattern in a shaded box. An analyst will get excited as the right shoulder or retracement forms in the far right part of that box. A trader will get interested when the pattern is broken at the *trend line* displayed in the chart. The trend line is called the *neckline of the reversal pattern.* The time to enter the trade (in this case, sell AMZN short) is when the market tries to test the trend line and fails. That is an immediate sell signal. The same formation develops at bottoms, and that pattern is called a *reverse head-and-shoulders pattern.* The time to buy is when the top of the trend line defining the neckline is tested. The market fails to break down through the trend line, and traders scramble to buy as fast as they can.

The gray box can be measured to define a price target. Take the height of the range in the box and project the same measurement from the black arrow to form an equality swing target. This is the same idea that was used to project a new high by employing a Fibonacci extension of 61.8 percent, equality or 100 percent, a 138.2 percent ratio, and a 161.8 percent proportional ratio to determine a new target from a pivot. In this example an equality measure is being discussed, but you also should calculate the other ratios. In this chart the lowest target would have been realized. If you reach an equality target projected from the black arrow, what should you do since you have other, lower targets? Get out. If you get a nice bounce to re-enter, fine, but that is a different trade with its own permission signals.

Figure 7.1   Weekly Chart for Amazon Showing a Head-and-Shoulders Pattern

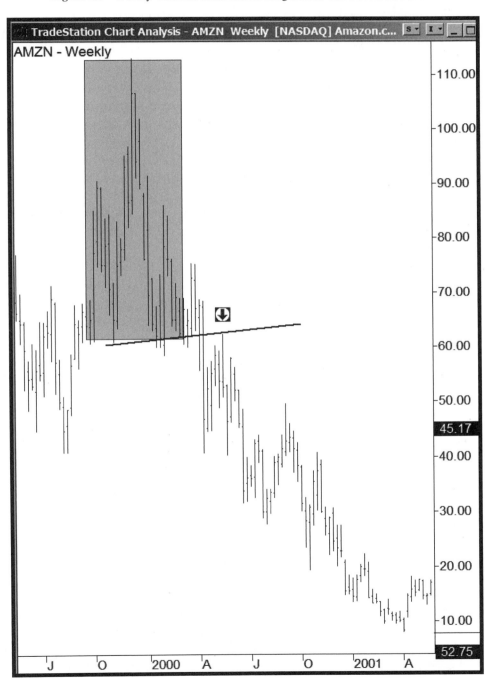

A key reversal into a retracement price target is a good place for reentry. The key is to bank the profits and leave something on the table for the next guy. This is one race that never ends, and you must pick your spots wisely and then execute your original strategy. In this example the original target is an equality move down from the range in the gray box relative to your entry signal.

The next entry signal is shown in Figure 7.2. This weekly chart for the Q's (the symbol is QQQQ), provides a perfect example of how a support line becomes a resistance line. The horizontal line was drawn to connect a key reversal price bar low (the upward pointing arrow) with the lows of the closing bars on the far left side of the chart. Yes, the actual price lows on the far left side break this line, but the majority of price action and all the market closing prices stay above it. This is important information. When the market tries to bounce into the underside of the line and fails with a key reversal directional signal, advanced traders will be all over this permission signal and scramble to sell the Q's short immediately.

Why do traders get so excited about these signals? They offer a low-risk entry point because the market may not, or should not, fully retrace the key reversal and break into a new high above the bar marked with the downward-pointing arrow. As a result, traders have an exit strategy at their backs. But what if the market just retraces the key reversal and knocks you out of your position and then reverses and dives south again, forming a key reversal with railway tracks? Sell short immediately. Your risk is limited, and you will not be betting more than 3 percent of your capital. You will have the ability to move freely as the opportunities develop. What if that happens a second time and the position has to be covered? Fine. It didn't work.

There is no other signal after the appearance of the railway track pattern to give you permission, and so you will not be suckered in again. You have to use your third trading position. Why the third position? You can buy, sell short, or stand aside. Stay on the sidelines and wait; watch like a hawk for the next signal and set up into a price target.

There is a way to increase your probability of being correct. Figure 7.3 uses two intra-day charts to demonstrate this technique. The foreign exchange (FOREX) market for Yen/$ is shown in this figure. The data looks the same for any market as far as the setup is concerned. You will be comparing two charts with a time ratio of 4:1. This chart shows intra-day data for 240-minute and 60-minute time intervals. (If your charting software doesn't allow you to plot 240 minutes, get new software. You need expert tools to make correct decisions. If your software cannot cut the mustard, get something that works.)

Figure 7.2   Weekly Chart for QQQQ Showing a Resistance Line

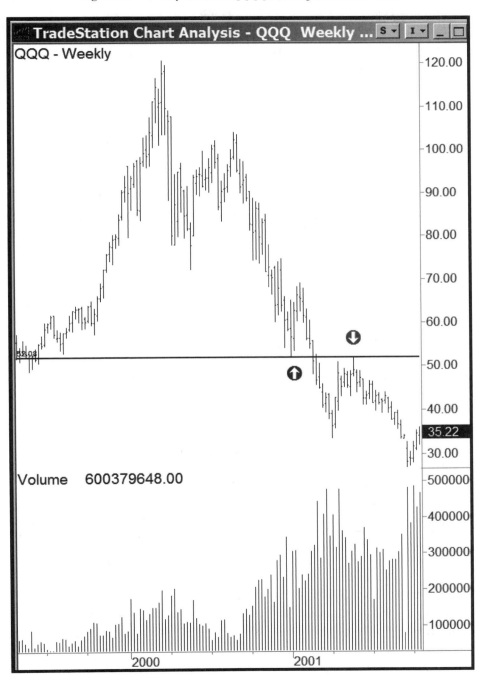

Figure 7.3 Intra-day Charts for Yen/$

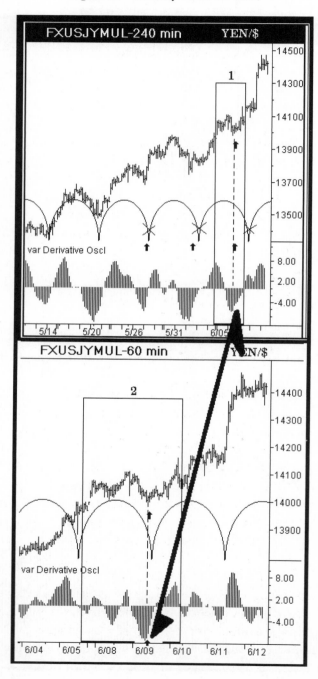

The approximate ratio of 4:1 works well because it fits month-to-week charts and week-to-day charts. There is enough of a difference to help filter bad signals out of your decision tree process.

In Figure 7.3, an oscillator is displayed under the data in both charts. You can find the formula in my book *Technical Analysis for the Trading Professional*. It is used here to show that any oscillator can be used. In this case it is the spread between two moving averages created on top of an oscillator. It is very smooth in its movement as a result.

The time comparison for consideration in the 240-minute chart has been highlighted in the box marked 1. The same time interval is highlighted in Box 2 in the 60-minute chart. In these two charts there is only one period when the oscillators in both charts are swinging upward after momentum lows. The fixed cycles are defined correctly in both charts, but the 240-minute chart cycles are out of phase at the critical point of comparison. The oscillators confirm each other and indicate that you need to buy immediately. If you are on support or a price target, the confirming signals in two time horizons provide you with the permission setup you need to enter a trade. Everything else in those boxes would cost you money as a result of lack of patience or because you did not use two charts.

Figure 7.4 shows the Dollar Index. This is a futures market. (I am not going back on my recommendation that you stay out of futures. These charts are screen captures I made of my own entry signals. You can find a library of charts on my Web site at www.aeroinvest.com.)

The weekly chart is on the left side and the daily chart is on the right side of the figure. The same oscillator is being used, but volume has been added under the indicator. The weekly Dollar Index chart shows the remains of a Fibonacci calculation that was made to determine support for the bounce. The daily chart also has resistance calculated to determine the top. The high marked "SELL" is the target zone, but the lines make the chart too busy for publication. The question is: Do I have permission to sell now that the market has reached the price target?

In both charts, you see that the oscillators have rolled over from extreme highs. In the daily chart, the volume under the price within the box is declining. This is all good stuff to take note of because you are gathering materials that paint the same picture. The oscillators confirm each other, the market was at a price target marking resistance, and volume was declining. That shows that the buy orders are drying up. I have other evidence, as the corrective rally into the "SELL" label is a specific Elliott Wave pattern. You can sell this market without that added piece of the permission puzzle. This chart is important because it shows how methods should add to or subtract from your weight evaluation. A fast way to

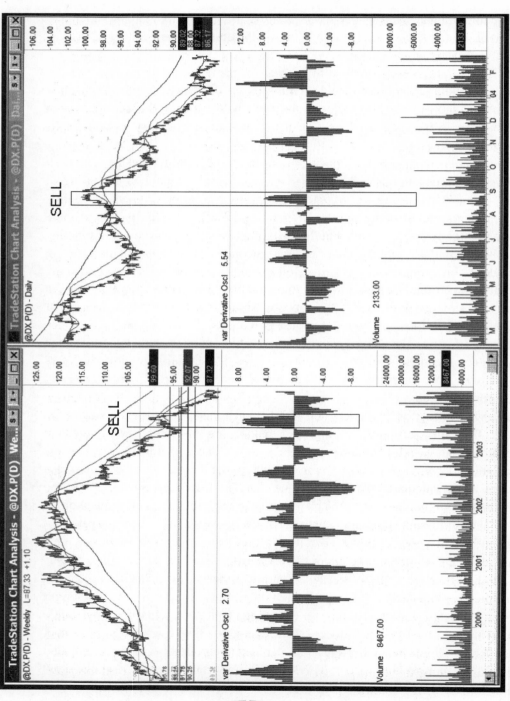

Figure 7.4 Weekly and Daily Dollar Index

mess yourself up is to have too many indicators that work in the same manner. Note that in this figure I have only one momentum indicator. Sometimes I use a second one to give me a warning that my indicator is misfiring or missing the boat, but more is never better.

Does this method work for investors who have a longer-horizon view? Figure 7.5 shows a Dow Jones Industrial Average (DJIA) monthly chart on the left and a weekly chart on the right. A support zone that defines a confluence zone of many tightly clustered targets has been shaded in gray in the monthly chart. When the DJIA reached that support zone, the oscillators gave you permission to buy.

There is another buy signal; it is easier to see in the weekly chart. The price action has two V-formations called a W-bottom. The second V-bottom is within the gray box in the weekly chart. It is higher than the first one. George Lane, the originator of the Stochastic Oscillator, used to show a picture of someone riding a bicycle from behind to get people to remember this setup. Also under the gray box is your price data volume. This time, the volume accompanying the second V-bottom is less than it is in the earlier price low. Note the spike behind the actual price low in the weekly chart. The price low is the decline to the left of the gray box. Now move back one more spike. The volume showed capitulation. The decline in the gray box is testing the spike low that displayed capitulation. The volume is considerably less than the volume two spikes back with capitulation *at the same low*.

Figure 7.6 shows a very simple yet compelling entry signal. It is a weekly chart for Amazon (AMZN). The key to understanding this chart is knowing where to draw the trend line. Note that the price lows are not connected; this trend line connects the majority of bar lows. It starts from a secondary retracement, not the actual price bottom, and passes through an area that connects the places where the majority of bars begin or where the strongest bars that move upward begin. This is often the key angle to know. This chart shows that AMZN tried to return to the high and failed right at this trend line. (Most of the time, the critical trend lines require you to use your smarts.) Secondary starting points from early corrections in a new trend are invaluable. This is one of the key points identified by W. D. Gann. If you have knowledge about the Elliott Wave Principle, you can use the ending of a corrective second wave.

Figure 7.7 shows a weekly chart for the NASDAQ Q's. In 2003 a similar setup formed for a market bottom. The small spike upward in volume came after that signal. Many people knew that the jig was up and began buying on heavy volume. The volume on the trend line is lower than the volume that accompanied the price low in 2002. This is a confirming signal.

Figure 7.5 Monthly and Weekly Dow Jones Industrial Average

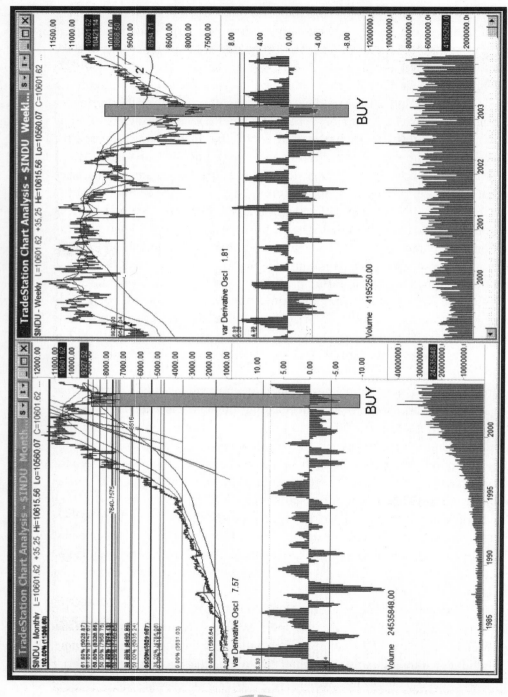

Figure 7.6   Weekly Chart for Amazon Showing a Trend Line

Figure 7.7   Weekly Chart for QQQQ

A weekly chart for Disney (DIS) is shown in Figure 7.8. When I started to explain comparisons of a recent pullback with ones that developed behind the most recent price low, some readers might have struggled with the concept. This chart will break down the concept further. A thin horizontal line has been drawn in this chart. The trend line is being tested, with a faint gray arrow highlighting that spot. Use the volume under the shorter vertical line to guide your eye. The test is sneaky this time. At the black arrow a longer bar under the arrow guides your eye to the lower volume. Study the horizontal line carefully. Track left to the low in 2001; it also has a capitulation spike in volume. Now look at the single price bar that is one to the right of this extreme low. The line has been drawn on this secondary retracement of the key reversal in 2001. The test developing at the black arrow is at exactly the same level. Retracements after major events are always important price levels of support or resistance.

Figure 7.9A is a monthly chart for Placer Dome, Inc. (PDG), a gold stock. In this chart I used a Stochastic Oscillator so that the correct setup of this indicator could be explained. Determine a fixed cycle and divide the cycle in half. The result will be the period interval used for the Stochastic Oscillator. In this chart the fixed cycle is 62. That is the spread or number of bars between price lows. However, there is no cycle notation in this chart, so how could one know? Look closely at the description after "Stochastic Slow," which reads "High, Low, Close, 31, 3, 3, 1, 20, 80." The first number in this listing is 31, and so the variable called %D was set at variable cycle of 31. Since you use half of the fixed cycle selected, you know that my period was 62 for this market. The visual for the cycle created can be viewed in Figure 7.9B.

Setting the period for this indicator is very important because the Stochastic Oscillator can swing back and forth very easily, and so the oscillations have to be in sync with the rhythms of the market to which the oscillator is applied. In Figure 7.9B a line has been drawn to guide your eye. It shows that the Stochastic Oscillator found resistance at the solid black dot in Figure 7.9A. The black dot with an arrow is testing the same line. In this case it can be said that resistance is becoming support. Here, volume has been added to the swings of the Stochastic Oscillator. Remember, it is relative volume that you are trying to determine. Therefore, I marked the high volume versus the low volume. The lower volume provides confirmation that the test above is giving you permission to buy this gold stock.

To clarify the use of the Stochastic Oscillator as a price target tool and an entry signal, look at Figure 7.10 (on page 139), which shows the housing stock Hovnanian (HOV) in a weekly time horizon. The gray area over the Stochastic Oscillator is a flutter pattern. The pattern develops when strong trends lock this indicator. The area

Figure 7.8 Weekly Chart for Disney (DIS)

Figure 7.9A   Cycle Analysis for Placer Dome Inc. (PDG)

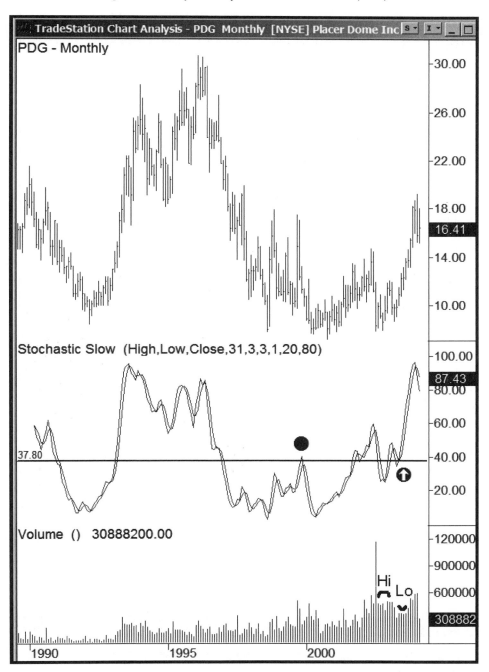

Figure 7.9B   Stochastic Interval Setup for Placer Dome Inc. (PDG)

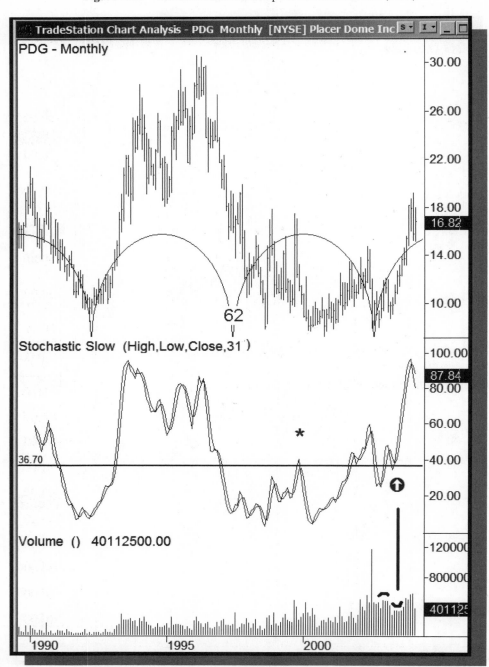

Figure 7.10   Weekly Chart for Hovnanian (HOV)

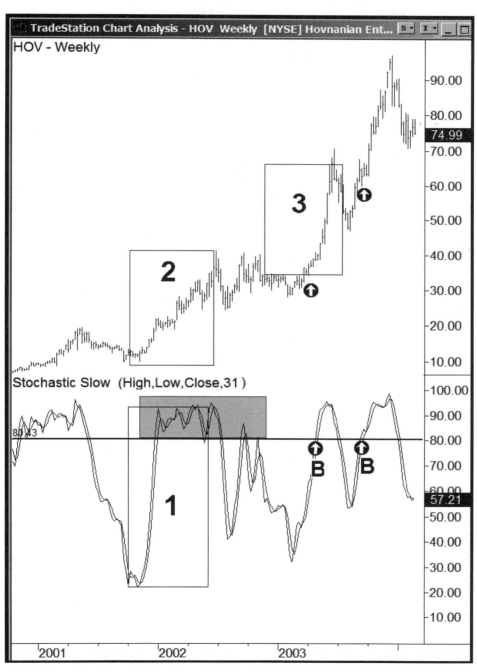

under the flutter is Box 1. It defines the range in which the indicator traveled from its last momentum low. In Box 2 the price range has been marked that unfolded during the period of time when the Stochastic Oscillator was tracking in Box 1.

This is the time to recall George Lane's instructions: "Do not sell a market as the Stochastic Oscillator crosses 80 after a flutter signal. Buy it when the indicator drives up through the 80 level again." The same box at position 2 is moved over to create Box 3. The height of the box is what is being discussed here, not the width, which implies time. The reentry level is at the first black arrow marked B. Another signal follows at the second arrow. However, note that the price target was realized if you bought at the first buy signal. At the second buy signal I did not draw a new box called 4. If you measure the second signal, you can see that the price target also was realized when it was projected upward from the entry price level of the second black arrow. However, you should use this method only for the first signal after the flutter pattern. The boxes drawn show internal proportions using geometry are being applied. If you measure the start of Box 2 to the middle of Box 3, then project this same range from the middle of Box 3, you will find the market highs reached the target of this measurement. Geometric proportions are extremely valuable and this stock HOV likely has serious trouble ahead as the long-horizon price objectives have been realized. All other signals that form in Stochastics in the shorter time horizon charts, such as daily will likely diverge and form sell signals until the oscillator can challenge the old oscillator extremes formed in 2001.

Figure 7.11 shows when to sell a stock short as the Stochastic Oscillator falls through the 20 level. A signal to sell short develops in a different manner here than it did in the last example. The Stochastic Oscillator does not display a flutter pattern in this chart window. It does, however, squiggle up into the 20 level of the Stochastic window where a black arrow and a large S meaning "sell short" is located. Why should you sell this time? Because the signal confirms what is happening in the price data. Study the horizontal line with a double boundary that runs across the page. I placed small arrows under this line to show how this area was selected.

The first black arrow (on the far right) pointing downward is marking a key reversal into this area, using a former area of support as resistance this time. This particular Stochastic Oscillator signal constitutes a very advanced read of this situation. It will take some experience to pick it out. The second S in the Stochastic Oscillator is similar to the first except that the indicator clearly is crossing down through the 20 level as opposed to just challenging it. The horizontal line on price at 31.44 (the label is on the far left of the line) has been set on the basis of the two small upward-pointing arrows. There is indeed a subtle art to technical analysis that requires attention to the smaller formations illustrated in this chart.

Figure 7.11   Weekly Chart for Amazon (AMZN) Showing When to Sell Short

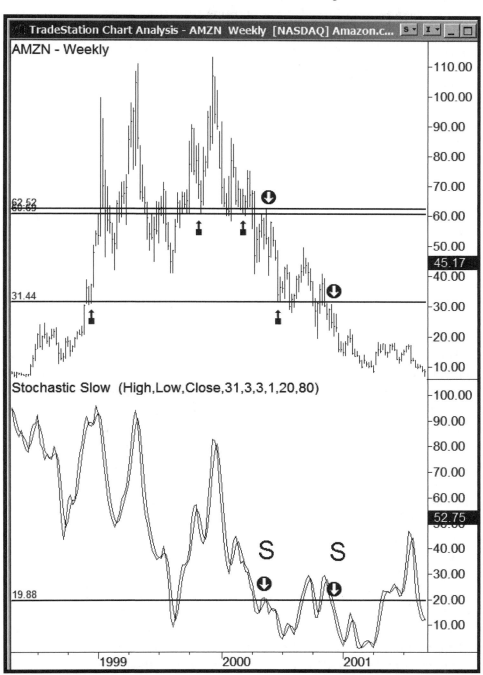

Figure 7.12 shows a weekly chart for the NASDAQ Q's setting up a geometric entry signal. The market produces a pullback that by itself seems insignificant. However, the lines in this chart show that the pullback was hugely important. Three geometric tools converge at that spot. You already understand the horizontal line and the trend line. The arc or ellipse in this chart is new. From the high, an ellipse tool has been drawn to connect a price low and a price retracement high. A high occurs in 2001 that becomes a failure. The line drawn is used as resistance by the market. This defines a geometric line with a sense of slope or speed attached to it. When the market is able to cross back through this arc, the character of the downtrend has changed. The method provides no measurement for a price projection.

Stochastic flutter produces another type of entry signal that is shown in Figure 7.13, which is a daily chart for the housing sector stock Hovnanian Enterprises (HOV). The flutter pattern is highlighted with a gray band on the indicator. In strong markets such as this rally in 2003, the Stochastic Oscillator flutter will end dramatically with any countertrend price move. The market can correct sideways in a tight price range and use time to alleviate the overbought or oversold excess pressure. In this chart there are two examples, and in both there is a Stochastic Oscillator plunge to the bottom of the computer frame. The first signal forms when a small W pattern develops in the indicator. The signal is viewed similarly to the pattern that forms in price. This is a double bottom in the momentum indicator. The rally resumes, and again a correction allows the indicator to plunge back to the bottom. This time, however, the indicator forms a bullish divergence signal. This gives you permission to enter when the correction has fallen to a price objective you determined beforehand. That is not a reason to buy the stock on the basis of this indicator signal alone.

Figure 7.14 shows HOV stock producing multiple sell signals in 2005. The monthly, weekly, and daily charts for HOV are displayed from left to right. This time the momentum indicator called the Relative Strength Index (RSI) is used. You can view these three charts as a tic-tac-toe board. *All three charts display and confirm bearish divergence.* In this case, sell it when all three time horizons scream the same message. This is rare and is a compelling signal when it forms. Plotted on top of the RSI are two simple moving averages, the same ones that are used on the price data above. They are used in the same manner, but they provide another dimension to the indicator that will be discussed more fully later in this chapter.

The monthly chart shows price swings marked 1 through 5. This is an introduction to a method called the Elliott Wave Principle. When five waves have developed, a decline back to wave 4 often occurs. The price swings marked 1, 3, and 5 are called

Figure 7.12   Weekly Chart for QQQQ Showing a Geometric Entry Signal

Figure 7.13   Daily Chart for Hovnanian Enterprises

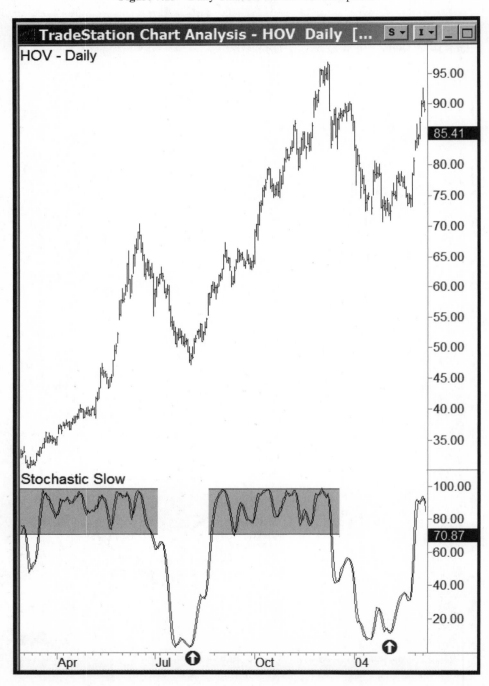

Figure 7.14 Hovnanian (HOV) Producing Multiple Sell Signals

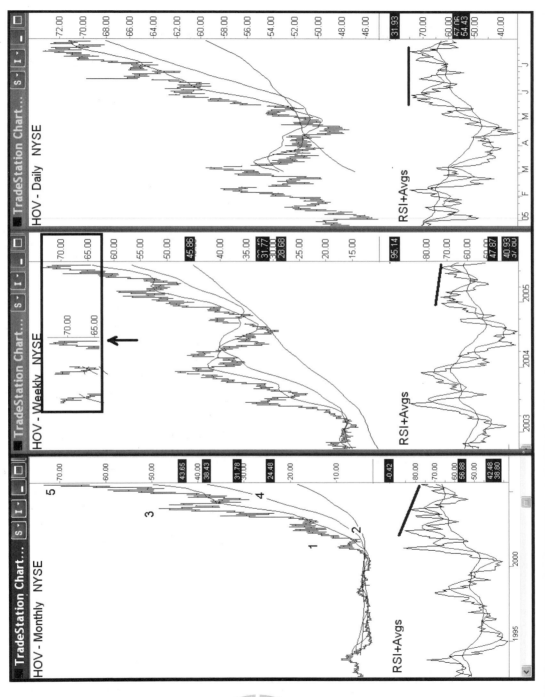

impulse waves. The corrections in the middle marked 2 and 4 are the corrective waves. If you look closely, the impulse waves can be subdivided further into their own sets of five waves. The swing from the low marked 2 to the high marked 3 is the clearest for studying the internal subdivision into five additional small waves.

The decline marked wave 4 never can overlap the top of wave 1. Another rule is to make sure that you never label swings that make wave 3 the shortest impulse wave. It can be equal to the distance traveled in wave 1 or wave 5 but never can be the shortest. These are a few of the basics, and the method actually is mapping out the psychology of the buyers and sellers of the market.

The weekly chart in Figure 7.14 shows the final price bar duplicated in a small insert at the top. It is comparing the recent decline with two other sharp corrections. This is a signal, as the recent drop exceeds the greatest single fall within the entire progression of the rally since the 1995 lows. This type of observation is very important, and so a chart with greater detail follows.

The story of HOV continues in Figure 7.15. This chart provides data for October 2006 and shows that the price decline from the signals in Figure 7.14 is sharp and unrelenting. The middle chart showing the weekly data has a black arrow highlighting the bounce. It is a signal in two ways to sell this market. The RSI retraces only to the underside of the momentum low marked with an upward-pointing arrow. Support has become resistance in the indicator this time. At the same time the signal is confirmed because the price data are failing to reach the moving average at the point marked with an arrow above the price move. The price data form another signal by transmitting a directional signal that was discussed earlier: a key reversal right under the arrow pointing at the price high.

When you look at all three time horizons and study the position of the RSI in this figure, you see that the monthly chart is oversold, the weekly chart is back at the high-risk trend line producing the second large price break in the same chart, and the daily data are forming a bearish divergence. This is normally what you see when a market decline is incomplete. A decent rebound has developed, but it is unlikely that it is the place where the entire decline will stop. Another low, and the weekly chart also could show bullish divergence adding weight to the monthly data. Read three charts together in each market you evaluate, over time horizons, across a like sector group, or across indexes such as the DJIA, the German DAX, and Japan's Nikkei.

Figure 7.16 is a daily chart for Caterpillar, Inc. (CAT). This rally allows for a deeper discussion of trading ranges. The range marked B defines the entire rally under consideration. The two bars marked C are the strongest 2 days within the entire move. Look for these very strong moves because they often define a 50 percent

Figure 7.15 October 2006 Charts for Hovnanian Enterprises

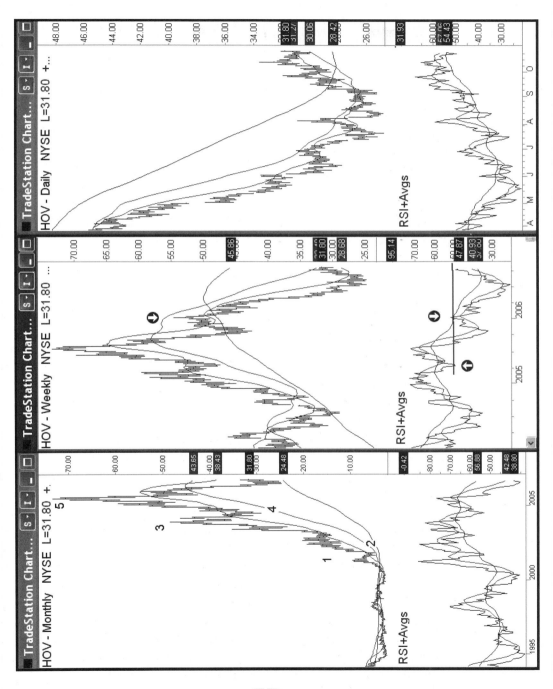

Figure 7.16   Daily Chart for Caterpillar Inc (CAT)

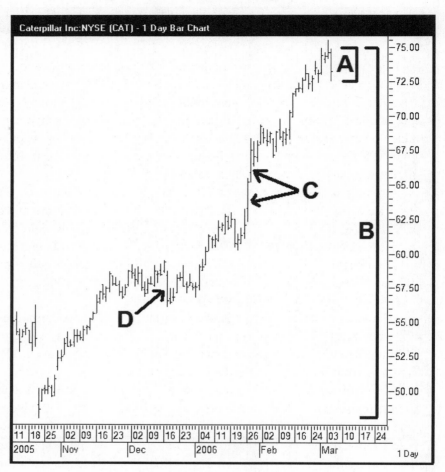

line within a developing swing. In this case, you would know from the strong bars to take the range from the bar marked D to the middle of C. Then you should project an equal move from C. In this case approximately $10 added to 65 produced a $75 price target. The two bars marked C should be given closer study. Know the exact high price and low price of each one. You should know the largest move up or down in a single day. The bar marked D is the largest single-day decline in the move, as you can tell by giving the data a quick glance. You need to know this so that you can detect a trend reversal signal. When the day's decline exceeds the largest single-day within the swing or exceeds the best day in the move as a range reference up or down, you will know that something significant may have occurred.

In Figure 7.14, the insert shows that the last decline in this weekly chart exceeds the two largest down weeks compared with the chart to the left. It is an extremely significant signal. Something indeed has changed when you see the follow-up breakdown in Figure 7.15.

Another signal is given when the market decline breaks below the price low of a prior corrective price swing and is unable to close over that low. As an example, using Caterpillar in Figure 7.16 as a visual reference, if prices fall below $71 and fail to close above $72, this is viewed as a signal because a larger move should follow to the downward side. You'll know this is a fairly early warning when you study Figure 7.15. Of course, the reverse is true after there has been a long decline and the market warns you that it is ready to reverse.

A very simple signal is shown in Figure 7.17, a weekly chart for the stock BSX. In 2003 the price action tested the old high three times. Floor traders say that when a resistance zone (or support) is tested three times, it probably will yield to the challenge. In this case the old high in 1999 is challenged, and the third time it blows upward into new highs. This is called a *market breakout,* and to be valid it must never break back down through the old high that served as resistance. It might trade through that high but never will close under it.

A group of traders called the Turtle Traders look for this specific formation. It works well when markets are trending, but when a market moves in a sideways range, the Turtle Traders are whipsawed horribly and become turtle soup. Don't use any signal by itself without having other reasons to take action.

A weekly chart for APC, an energy stock, is shown in Figure 7.18. This is a good chart for reviewing several concepts. The price low at $40 is marked with a large B and an upward-pointing arrow. This is a buy signal in a Fibonacci zone that contains two Fibonacci ratios derived from two different ranges. It is a major support zone because two different Fibonacci ratios cross the same price level. There are two touching arrows marked Z to ensure that you see the zone that formed. The APC stock falls to this target, and a buy signal develops at this zone. The RSI is giving you permission to buy because bullish divergence is present compared with prices making new lows. How far will this bounce go? You cannot answer that question by looking at this chart, but take a close look at the simple moving averages on top of the RSI. The spread is deemed to be negative because the faster, or shorter-period, average is positioned below the slower, or longer-period, average of the RSI. When the averages are negative, the bounce may be only a countertrend move upward. Another decline at least back to 42 would test the lows behind the low marked B.

To add to your confidence and market opinion in the longer-horizon charts, you also need an opinion on the oil market itself and just rely on the oil stock to base

Figure 7.17   Weekly Chart for BSX

Figure 7.18   Weekly Chart for APC

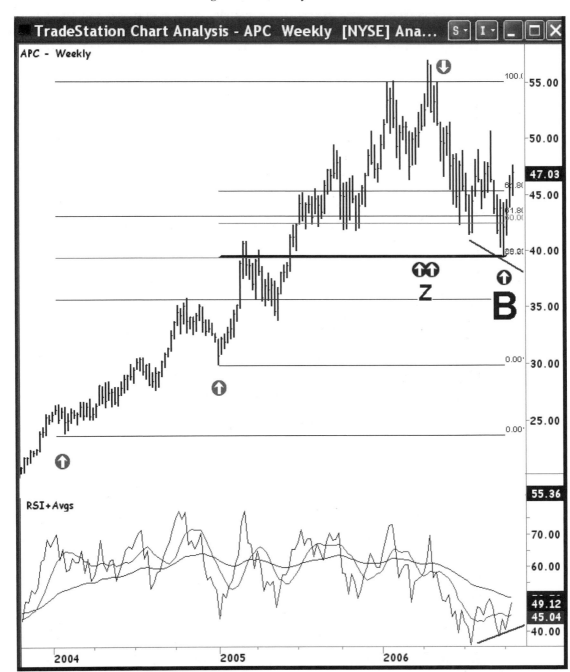

your analysis. You want to know if a decline in oil is complete. You also would like to know if stocks turn before and hence lead the oil market or lag it. You will find that stocks often lead commodities. This is a lot to learn, but you are using the correct comparisons and know the basics of price projections.

What is missing? *You need to know at what price your opinion about APC is wrong* and it will not rally with your expectations. A Fibonacci line just above $35 is shown. If you trace the same line to the left, you will see that it marks an old price high in 2004. In fact, it is the price high in 2004. Thus, the market cannot close below this line, but it can swing under it briefly. Keep stops beneath this area. Stops protect you from incurring massive losses. They also define your risk exposure versus your reward as a risk-to-reward ratio. If you buy at 440 and hold stops just under $35 and expect a rally back to the old highs just over $55, you are working a risk-to-reward ratio of 1:3. That means that for a dollar at risk there is the potential to make $3. Do not step into the market for less than that. What is the point of risking a dollar to make only a dollar? It makes little sense to take the risk at a ratio of 1:2 as well. Always define where your market opinion is proven to be wrong before you enter a trade. That way you have a plan and must act on it. If you know the risk-to-reward ratio, you also can calculate the amount of money you can risk. Do not risk more than 3 percent of your trading account on a single idea. Do not risk more than 10 percent of your account at any time while you are learning. You may be thinking that this amount is too small, but this is a professional approach to risk management. You should not be using margin at all when you are learning or have emotional concerns about a loss. This is a game of mental health, and it is important to trade from a position of strength. Those who do not learn this lesson trade in order not to lose, but that is exactly what happens to them. You have to know how to trade to win, which is a very different mind-set.

When the market begins to make a strong rally after a buy signal, it is important to protect your profits by reducing your risk exposure. Some people use a technique called a trailing stop.

Figure 7.19 shows one way to move trailing stops under corrective swings. Other ways might include using a short-period moving average under which to hide stops. Some people use something called volatility bands. This is a method that involves using the standard deviation, and it defines an upper channel and a lower channel. In my opinion, all these methods are poor techniques for risk management because you have to give so much of your profit back before you exit. I favor using Fibonacci zones as they develop from each new swing. Keeping stops under the major confluence zones such as the entry signal in Figure 7.18 allows you to give less money back because you react much sooner than you do with the trailing stop

Figure 7.19   Weekly Chart for Caterpillar Showing How to Move Trailing Stops

technique. Everyone finds his or her own comfort zone, and some traders use similar indicators in shorter time horizons to exit. I do not hang around for a confirmation. If the market looks overdone and you are very near the target area, take the money!

Quiz for Chapter 7

1. A reversal pattern in an uptrend with a rally, a correction, a rally into new price high, a correction, and then a third rally attempt that fails near the highs of the first swing upward is called a:

   a. Hook-and-reversal pattern

   b. Head-and-shoulders pattern

   c. Price failure

   d. Distribution top

   e. Triple threat reversal pattern

2. In the pattern described in question 1, two corrections fall between the three rally swings. A trend line drawn to connect the lows of the corrections is a:

   a. Specific trend line called a neckline

   b. Resistance line

   c. Double trough

   d. Specific trend line called a reversal line

   e. Double-V pattern

3. The three ratios of greatest interest in a Fibonacci extension are:

   a. 38.2 percent, 61.8 percent, and 75 percent

   b. 61.8 percent, 75 percent, and 100 percent

   c. 38.2 percent, 61.8 percent, and 100 percent

   d. 61.8 percent, 100 percent, and 161.8 percent

   e. 100 percent, 138.2 percent, and 161.8 percent

4. The three ratios of greatest interest in using a Fibonacci extension in a bear market are:

   a. 38.2 percent, 61.8 percent, and 75 percent

   b. 61.8 percent, 100 percent, and 161.8 percent

   c. 61.8 percent, 75 percent, and 100 percent

d. 38.2 percent, 61.8 percent, and 100 percent

    e. 100 percent, 138.2 percent, and 161.8 percent

5. A market decline bounces back to the underside of a resistance line and forms a key reversal. Why should a trader be particularly interested in this development?

    a. It is a reversal pattern at resistance

    b. It is a reversal pattern at resistance with confirmation

    c. It is a reversal pattern at resistance offering a low-risk entry

    d. It is a reversal pattern offering a low-risk entry

    e. It is a confirmed reversal pattern at support

6. Volume added to the bottom of a chart under the price data will:

    a. Always be of value at a market top

    b. Always spike when a major market washout develops

    c. Diverge from prices before a market reversal

    d. A and C

    e. B and C

7. When you compare two charts of different time periods, the ratio that is most valuable is:

    a. An 88-minute chart versus a 22-minute chart (4:1)

    b. A 60-minute chart versus a 10-minute chart (6:1)

    c. An 88-minute chart versus an 11-minute chart (8:1)

    d. A 30-minute chart versus a 15-minute chart (2:1)

    e. A 60-minute chart versus a 5-minute chart (12:1)

8. Trend lines always should:

    a. Connect price lows to price highs

    b. Connect the majority of bar lows

    c. Connect exact price lows within an uptrend

    d. Connect exact price highs within an uptrend

    e. Connect the majority of bars displaying key reversals

9. When volume is lower on a second decline and price fails to make a new low, this is called:

    a. Volume divergence

    b. Price divergence

    c. Confirmation

    d. Bullish divergence

    e. Bearish divergence

10. The correct method for setting the period interval for a Stochastic Oscillator is to:

    a. Use the quote vendor's setup until you learn more

    b. Determine a fixed-cycle interval at price lows and use half that interval in the indicator

    c. Use a 14-period interval in all Stochastic Oscillator charts

    d. Determine a fixed-cycle interval at price lows and use that interval in the indicator

    e. Use 18 because George Lane favored that approach in all his chart work.

CHAPTER 8

Mirror, Mirror on the Wall

"You can only win one for the Gipper...once," wrote former Boston Celtics president and NBA legend Red Auerbach in his book *MBA: Management by Auerbach*. He was referring to the old Ronald Reagan movie recounting the story when the dying football player George Gipp asks Knute Rockne, Notre Dame's legendary coach, to tell the team to win the big game "for the Gipper."

In his book Auerbach expressed his thoughts about that approach. His view was that you can rally for a particular cause only once, leaving the question: What do I do the second time? He could ask his team to win one for the Gipper only one time, and then he had to find out what motivated each individual to keep them all producing. He strongly believed that it is not possible to motivate a team or a group. The key is to understand the motivation for each individual on the team.

Understanding Your Motivation

Do you know what motivates you to enter the markets? If you believe that it is simply the money, there will come a time when you share the problem of some professional athletes: It becomes hard to continue day after day. Chasing money can run your motivation gas tank down to empty. When you look beneath the surface, your needs often reveal that money is a secondary motive.

The secret of becoming a good trader is to know yourself. Do you know what your strengths and weaknesses are in stressful situations? Trading will bring out your best and worst qualities because there is no place to hide. This aspect of trading and investing will make or break you. Active participation in the markets forces each trader to look in the mirror and examine his or her character. What makes this so hard is the fact that most people experience behavioral changes when the stakes increase. Simply stated, you will process information differently when you are trading as opposed to being on the sidelines.

An individual's motivation comes from loving what he or she does. Some people seem to love the quest to find the perfect system. System hopscotch is a symptom of being in the business for investigative research. The problem with that approach is finding a way to know when to stay with the tools that work and resist changing merely because you've found something new. By developing a history with your methods, you add depth of understanding to your trades. Jumping to a new method because it seems better without having a specific reason to make the change is a recipe for disaster. You will never know how to make a decision with confidence as you will come across conflicting information.

Is something different attracting you to trading? Is it the constant development of a global puzzle that needs to be solved? Is it the intellectual challenge? Is it the challenge coupled with the need to "beat the game"? When I began my career, a statement was made that no one in my firm wanted S&P futures because that was the toughest game in town. That was enough for me to want to get into S&P futures. If it was deemed tough, I wanted to conquer it and prove that I could survive.

Perhaps you have a more fundamental need, such as security. Some people trade to satisfy their need for respect. The question "What motivates you?" is not an easy one to answer.

Trading Accountability

Good traders tend to have certain common traits. Those traders all have one thing in common: They are accountable for their own actions—not just some of their actions but all of them. You make the decision about the timing, the methods used to make a decision, the time to step in, the method used to determine when to enter and exit, the people you associate with and how much control they should be given, and so on. The fact that the kids are making noise when you are trading from home, the fact that your broker swayed you to do something against your better judgment, the fact that you got a rotten fill, the fact that you are coming down with the flu—all these are explanations that elicit the same response: Tough. Suck it up, change it, or do not trade on those days.

This process is a rite of passage, and every trader has to learn the same lessons. Blame is a cop-out that lets people tell themselves that they are not responsible. It is vital to a trader's success to recognize that everyone gets a bad fill sometimes, everyone has off days, and everyone must be accountable because you cannot change what you do not acknowledge.

If you have distractions at home when you trade, you have to establish rules and define a private space that is to be invaded only in the event of fire or death. Professional traders often start with a space no bigger than a broom closet on an island of traders sitting shoulder to shoulder. You have to be strong enough not to care what the trader beside you is doing. Traders have to develop a mind-set that is called *entering the zone*.

The zone is a state of mind that is known widely among athletes. It is a state of hyperfocus. When a person is in this state of extreme concentration, everything seems to become acute and the perception of time slows down. There is nothing in the zone except total focus on your computer screen and the multiple market elements that require your attention. If you are an investor and are not watching a position actively around the clock, you are not focused. Your game face and total attention are required as you develop your plan and select your market timing or system for stock selection. If you cannot find some "private trader time" within your work schedule and in the context of your family commitments, do not trade.

Trading Stress

What about the times when you have a position on and don't feel so great? What about the times when you have to make a fast trip out of town and have positions on that are doing great? Travel or illness will cause the greatest losses. You will have poor judgment when you are sick, and it seems that the worst things happen when people travel because they cannot do anything about the problems. The stress is not worth it. Close out of those positions when you travel or become ill. If they are very long-term positions, at least move the stops up closer to protect yourself.

Trading Performance

The emotional swings you experience in trading rarely are as high or low as what you experience in everyday life. As a result, investors have a tendency to base their self-worth on their trading performance. It is not entirely their fault that they do this because people are programmed from childhood to judge themselves on the basis of their performance in a quest for perfection.

People are told from childhood not to make a mistake. At school everything is set up to lead to perfection. However, perfection does not exist, and so the conditioning that starts in childhood is a path that disempowers people. If people are not perfect, they feel that they must work harder to focus on that goal. This messes people up when they face the markets, because the markets are always right and always available. Successful traders learn how to step into a race that has no finish line and how to feel accomplished in an arena where the results cannot be recorded in black and white.

Mental Balance

Mental balance is a trader's greatest asset in reading the markets. If your own life is in harmony you can focus and listen to your inner voice. Your greatest friend or enemy will be yourself. Chapter 11 contains thoughts that may help you understand human nature and improve your trading.

KNOW YOUR INNER POLES

When we are in an emotional state of balance we are neither extremely negative nor positive. We just go with the flow of life. The same poles we carry within us apply to our market intuition. Some charts will raise your inner positive pole, and some will add to your negative pole. Neither pole is good or bad; they both just are. When the positive pole is so extreme that you cannot take the feeling any longer, you buy something; when the negative pole is at an extreme, you sell. I once asked an audience of highly skilled traders, "What happens when all that we know and all that we have gained in market experience leads to a condition where we feel nothing?" Experienced traders know when to sit on the sidelines because the poles have canceled each other out.

There are many ways in which people's inner poles can be damaged. For me, September 11, 2001, was a personal tragedy because I used to work on the 104th floor of the North Tower, and, like so many in the business, I lost friends, colleagues, and a physical place where my memories and history formed. We all had to deal with this pain on many different levels, but the trauma of 9/11 may be overshadowed if you have experienced the painful loss of a child or a parent. Day-to-day pressures such as an increase in financial responsibility, job relocation, and injury or illness all take a toll on a person's inner balance. If you say that it is okay and move on, you effectively have created an inner block. These are the kinds of things that will change your response rate to the markets and the way you perform when chaos unfolds on the screen. Good traders are always trying to find a place of peace that serves as an inner balance point. They know they need a secure place to start from when they walk up to the plate to take a swing at the markets.

On one occasion I worked with a local horse whisperer, Bruce Anderson, who used a well-coiled lariat to prove a point. He asked me to toss the rope *toward* a post about 14 feet away. I naturally wanted to ensure that it made it to the post, but I tossed it about 10 feet *past* the post. Bruce asked, "Do you always have to over achieve to feel you reached the goal?" Yikes! He was right. Then to complete the task, or "picture," as Bruce called it, he asked me to coil the rope again so that it was in a condition in which he originally handed the rope to me. I had to struggle since the lariat has a resin to keep the coils in place. The rope twisted and had tension. I tried to force it and wrap the rope around my elbow and hand. Stuck. The rope had me trapped. So I took it apart and slowly coiled the rope with each coil releasing the stress of inner tension. Well, all but one coil that is. Bruce asked me to throw the rope a second time. The rope developed a massive tangled knot in the middle and missed the chair by a foot. However, it had been tossed in the correct direction. Bruce asked, "How do you feel right now?" "Horrible and embarrassed," I replied. "Why?" Bruce asked. "Because I failed to hit the post." "Ah, but was not the task to toss the rope toward the post? You have increased the difficulty for yourself once again by expecting to hit the post as well. How's that working for you?"

DON'T WAIT FOR PERFECTION

Do you see the similarity between this story and trading? Performing a simple task like that can help all traders see the pressures they put on themselves in the markets. Not only do traders want the market to go in their direction, it has to hit their target exactly before they realize that they should bank the profits. The fact that the rope had a big knot in the middle on the second toss also added pressure. Traders see this in the market when it decides to create a consolidation where they do not expect one to form. But if it never challenges one's stops and moves toward the target, has it created any less of a profit?

If you feel you failed, that will affect the way you interact with the market as you find that the target was shy $0.75—a mere 75 cents. As the market pulls back, you take no action because you may need the next push into the "post" to prove yourself right. Therefore, in this situation you may freeze. We are a culture of overachievers who need validation for a task well past the true parameters of completion before we can feel satisfaction. We are hard on ourselves, and the response comes in the form of three alternative actions: We freeze, flee, or fight. When the market comes very close to your target, take the money and run! Don't wait for perfection. Unfortunately, perfection is what people were taught to expect, and it messes everyone up when it comes to trading markets.

Trading psychology is fascinating. Chapter 11 takes another look at this since trading psychology is the primary reason traders win or lose.

Traits of Successful Traders

Successful traders have certain common personality traits. How would you rate yourself in terms of the 10 descriptions that follow?

1. They are fiercely independent.

2. They have a commitment to stick to a task or solve a problem for days longer than what most people would consider possible.

3. They have discipline without anguish. Time passes by effortlessly as repetitive tasks are performed without emotion or stress.

4. They take responsibility for their own actions.

5. They learn from their mistakes.

6. They have the ability to release tension.

7. They have a sense of humility. This may seem out of place, but as time goes on, you will find that the markets are very humbling. The best traders know not to let their egos get out of control.

8. They have realistic expectations.

9. They know that there are times when they should not trade because there is nothing to gain when the market is going sideways.

10. They have the ability to act on what they see. It is not enough to recognize an opportunity; you have to act on it in order to put it in the bank.

Quiz for Chapter 8

1. Money motivates everyone to trade markets.
    a. True
    b. False

2. Five momentum oscillators are better than two momentum oscillators to get confirmation, establish probability, and break a tie if there is a conflict.
    a. True
    b. False

3. You are trading at home, and the fact that the kids are making noise explains why your trade is not going well.
    a. True
    b. False

4. Your broker recommended stock XYZ, and you acted on that recommendation. It did not go as planned, but that is all right because it was not really your trade.

   a. True

   b. False

5. The phrase "entering the zone" is a sports term that describes players who are at the top of their game, in the moment, and fully focused.

   a. True

   b. False

6. Using end-of-day data only provides sufficient information for an investor interested in holding positions over a period of weeks.

   a. True

   b. False

7. You may experience the greatest loss on open positions when you experience a market event rather than when you are sick or traveling.

   a. True

   b. False

8. Traders should not base their self-worth on their trading performance.

   a. True

   b. False

9. Good traders often:

   a. Are fiercely independent

   b. Have the ability to sit and solve problems for days without interruption

   c. Learn from their mistakes

   d. Have a sense of humor

   e. All of the above

10. Good traders often:

    a. Take responsibility for their losses

    b. Exercise daily to improve their conditioning

    c. Work alone on their market skills

    d. Are disciplined in recording what went right as well as what could be improved with further study

    e. All of the above

CHAPTER 9

How to Develop Your Own System

Earlier chapters discussed ways to project prices, define support and resistance, and use indicators to determine how the market will behave at critical price levels. At this stage you should ask: What will it take to develop my own systematic approach to analyzing the market? Without guidance you will run into trouble. There are many methods to consider: Analyses of geometry, momentum, sentiment, and breadth are only a few of them. To prevent you from falling into a trap, here is some cautionary advice.

Investors tend to collect momentum and behavioral or sentiment indicators like baseball cards. One trader asked for my help after he had collected more than 170 oscillators; he was proud of the fact that he knew everything about all of them. There was one problem: He didn't know when to make a trade. Because he had so much information to sift through, his positive and negative poles were overloaded. The real problem was that he never had enough confidence to trade because he had so many indicators that he could find reasons to doubt any decision he made. If you trade not to lose, that will happen. You have to enter the market with the intention to win. In this business, it is called analysis paralysis when someone constantly tries to find another method to boost his or her confidence. The self-doubt and hesitation can be extremely costly. If you do not know how to follow a game plan for researching indicators and do not develop a trading strategy that matches your personality, your efforts can become redundant and ineffective.

Market Analysis Methods

For analytic purposes you want to develop three non-correlated market analysis approaches. Using two oscillators, such as a fast stochastic indicator and a slow moving-average convergence divergence (MACD) indicator, provides only one market analysis approach, not two. The two studies together contribute to the generation of one market signal when they are used correctly. My method has a few parts. I use the *relative strength index* (RSI) and the spread between averages that was covered in Chapter 4. When used in conjunction with the Fibonacci price analysis that was covered in Chapter 3 to define support and resistance levels, those indicators produce one signal.

The second method that I use is called the *Elliott Wave Principle*. This is a method of mapping market sentiment that helps identify the stage at which the majority of participants currently are within the selling or buying cycle. Like a business cycle, markets have stages any person with an MBA can identify with. There are early market participants, early and late majority participants, and laggards. As the market matures, the different buying behaviors that are seen in business cycles play out similarly in repeating market patterns. This is a method that is mentioned here only as an example of a non-correlated approach to technical analysis that does not incorporate momentum oscillators when it is used alone. The Wave Principle requires geometry design skills because it involves analyzing market swings to consider their balance and proportions.

My third method is called *Gann analysis*. You were introduced to it briefly near the end of Chapter 6, which covered cycles. It helps me answer the question "When will something happen?" It also has a very advanced price analysis component that helps me determine which price target among several has the highest probability of being the final target before a move begins. The second and third methods may not be your preferences, but all three are very different, and clearly they are non-correlated.

Each method may have several components, but I am always acutely aware that the components simply add a degree of probability to the three final signals that my favored analysis approaches provide. You should have three non-correlated market signals or opinions and no more. Together these three different approaches provide a strong market opinion when they agree. (This plan will help you avoid the pitfalls of developing 170 oscillators that basically do the same thing.)

It is possible to tweak an indicator to the point where it turns into something else. For example, one individual altered the formula for the RSI to such an extent that it looked and behaved just like a Stochastic Oscillator. Use only the Stochastic Oscillator if that is the oscillation sensitivity you want your momentum oscillators to look like. What is most important is staying with a method so that you can learn its characteristics in various market conditions. Don't jump around exploring different methods. Make changes very slowly after you have seen a new method's performance in real-time market scenarios, not just by back-testing setups with historical data.

Automating signals is a huge mistake unless you have a tremendous number of markets to track and use the automated signals as a flag that alerts you to begin your own work because certain criteria were met. The early chapters advised you to study chart internals to learn how a market functions and how it respects a technique. Ignoring these variations is perhaps the primary reason "system" traders continue to be blown out of the market in large numbers when the market moves away from a strong trend.

Methods of Analysis of Momentum, Breadth, and Sentiment

The list that follows describes methods that study market momentum, breadth, and sentiment. A trader who developed momentum analysis and then added breadth or sentiment indicators would have two non-correlated methods. The key is to know what the underlying source of data is, based on factors such as price, volume, and sentiment. All the methods listed here are used to indicate whether the market has enough steam to plow through resistance or support zones or whether it is overextended and about to reverse.

Here are several ways to track market extremes and market behavior.

Advance/Decline Ratio. An analytic method widely used by stock analysts and brokers. It is a ratio of advancing shares to declining shares for the period that is plotted. Consider this an analysis tool and not a market timing tool.

Advisory Sentiment Index. An analytic measure that indicates how many analysts are giving buy recommendations versus sell recommendations. The idea here is that markets move against the majority of traders.

ADX and ADXR. This indicator is a trend oscillator. Regardless of whether the market is trending upward or downward, the indicator will advance. (Some people love it. I have strong feelings against it because it lags a market move to an extreme degree.)

Bollinger Bands. A set of bands plotted above and below the market to define extremes. Bollinger Bands allow price to run higher or lower than the volatility bands without meaning in strong trends.

Commitment of Traders Index. A sentiment indicator compiled by the futures exchanges. This index measures the buying and selling activity of professionals versus that of traders with small public positions. It assumes that the professionals will be right when the small retail traders have bet the opposite side to an extreme. (This is correct, but the timing is horrible as the extreme can be in place for many months.)

Directional Movement Index. You will encounter this tool as a separate indicator, but it is required to calculate the ADX and ADXR indicators, which are averages applied to this index.

Insider Buy-Sell Ratio. A sentiment ratio based on insider trading of stock. It assumes that the insider is trading on information the general public cannot see. (Do not waste your time on this information. The past performance of this indicator suggests that even the insiders are in the dark.)

Keltner Channels. These channels are another type of volatility band that defines a range above and below the market. This is a very popular method for traders who do not have price projection techniques in their arsenal.

Large Block Ratio. A stock barometer that measures activity in block trades. When you trade "in size," you are trading in thousand-share blocks. Those trades are recorded, and collective totals are analyzed to determine professional activity.

Market Profile. A unique display developed by Peter Steidlmayer. It shows the volume of buying and selling at specific price points. It was developed for trading futures and is a real-time display of information.

McClellan Oscillator and McClellan Summation Index. Both of these indicators are measures of sentiment.

Odd Lot Balance Index, Odd Lot Purchases/Sales, Odd Lot Short Ratio, and Odd Lot Short Sales. An odd lot is a stock order in an odd amount less than 100 shares. Thus, a trade of 64 shares is an odd lot trade that probably came from the public sector. Odd lot statistics are compared with those for block trades. (This is the stock trader's answer to the future trader's Commitment of Traders data.)

Offset Moving Average. This method provides a way to place trailing stops as the lag in a normal moving average gives back a lot of the profit. By artificially shifting the average forward, it changes the timing.

Parabolic or Stop and Reversal. This is a method that is used to warn a trader about trend reversals. (It is a terrible trading tool that will chop your account into small pieces.)

Percent Industry Groups Rising/Falling. Data on individual stocks or on like stock groups. It indicates the market breadth by showing whether a wide array of sectors are advancing or falling versus a select group producing the move within the stock indexes.

Percentage Bands. You can create a range around the current trading price by adding a fixed percentage above or below the market. You also have the flexibility to use the closing, low, or high price for the calculations.

Pivot Point Channels. A method of interest to futures traders because it used to be widely known on the floors of the exchanges. (I am not sure how effective the targets are now that electronic trading has taken over.)

Premium Ratio. Futures are analyzed on a cash basis market. Sometimes the cash and futures markets develop an arbitrage imbalance that traders who focus on these small ripples move in to benefit from. You will encounter this ratio only with futures and intraday trading.

Put-call Ratio. A ratio plotted as an oscillator derived from option trading. The ratio of puts-to-calls on the S&P 100 OEX Index is perhaps the most commonly used.

Ratio of AMEX Volume to NYSE Volume. It is possible to compare the trading activity between exchanges. The American Stock Exchange has midsize capital stocks in its index versus the large capitalization companies in the New York Stock Exchange. The ratio is an indication of which segment of the market is leading or lagging. (I find it more effective to chart the top eight mutual funds for a specific capitalization focus.)

Relative Strength Comparison. A common method of analysis is to compare the performance of a stock to that of a sector or a sector to another sector or index. This defines which sector will outperform the other and which is expected to underperform.

Volatility. A market that keeps moving upward day after day is a *low*-volatility market. *High*-volatility markets are ones that swing back and forth; they are choppy or form sharp rever sols.

Volume Oscillator. An indicator that keys off volume data.

These are certainly not all the indicators and methods that measure momentum, breadth, or sentiment. However, this is a representative list.

The bottom line for all these studies is this: Momentum and sentiment extremes can tell you when there is a high probability that the market will reverse, but not one of the formulas or indicators in this list can tell you how far the market will move once it changes direction.

Why do you want to go to the trouble of learning about all these methods? It is necessary to know how a market may react to the key price targets and levels of market support and resistance that are identified by these tools. Your price projection methods will tell you how far a market may move. Therefore, these studies and price projection methods go hand in hand. Using price projection methods alone is like seeing a train station and having no idea whether the train will stop or go on to the next one. Momentum, breadth, and sentiment indicators tell you that this is not only the stop but the end of the trip and that the train will return.

Three Schools of Thought

The first of the three approaches that will be discussed is to mathematically study relative opening and closing prices. The premise is that markets that are weak will close below their opening for the period being charted and that strong markets will close the period higher than they opened. Momentum indicators as a group function in this manner. The various momentum formulas and resulting squiggles that you can add to your charts all use this underlying premise to measure market strength or weakness.

A second school of thought holds that price data alone cannot tell the whole story no matter what kind of indicator you develop to study prices. Technicians who use this approach follow methods known as market breadth indicators. They rely on formulas that are used to study volume and market activity rather than price data alone. For example, they need to know how many New York Stock Exchange (NYSE) stocks are advancing and declining in the same time period. (Market breadth indicators apply to equities, but they are better for analysis than at giving timely trading signals.)

Futures markets analyze both *open interest* and volume. Open interest offers another level of transparency. For example, in futures markets, high volume alone is not necessarily a good thing. Open interest is a number that indicates how many new futures contracts have been created and remain open before the agreements behind the contracts have to be filled. The contract date that forces the holder to deliver or buy the underlying commodity is the delivery date. For example, every contract that is open has to be closed before the delivery date so that you can avoid receiving 20 boxcars of cattle in the garage of your apartment building in Manhattan. If you are short on the delivery date, you are obligated to buy the 20 cars of cattle and deliver them to a specific location defined by the exchange.

Less than 3 percent of all futures traded become bound by the terms of delivery. Therefore, if you do not understand how a futures contract legally binds you to an agreement, you probably should not trade them.

If it is not cattle, it could be any other commodity. The key here is to know that high volume that is accompanied by declining open interest is a warning that money is being extracted from the market; when this happens, analysts become concerned about a trend reversal. In contrast, when open interest is increasing along with volume, this indicates that new contracts are being agreed to, and that confirms that new money is being committed. For a trend to be sustained, new money must enter a market.

The third school of thought is where market behaviorists reside. These technicians develop formulas to monitor the buying and selling activity of the bearish crowd versus that of the bullish crowd. They also analyze the activity of commercial traders versus that of the general public. The underlying premise is that the general public or retail sector is usually wrong and the smart money is usually in the hands of the people in the know: the professional and commercial traders. These technicians also think that if a majority of market participants become overly weighted on one side of the spectrum, whether bullish or bearish, the market will find a way to do damage to the greatest number of participants. This method of analysis is called *sentiment analysis*.

STUDY OF PRICE DATA

In Chapter 4 there was a brief discussion of the oscillator called the MACD. Consider the MACD that is plotted under "Stochastics+Avgs" in Figure 9.1, which

Figure 9.1   Weekly Chart for a Vanguard Fund

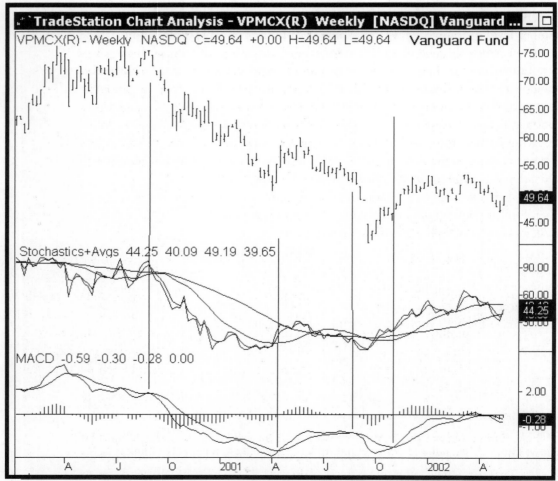

is a weekly chart for a Vanguard fund. The fund bottomed in October 2002, and so analysts who used this indicator would have experienced another swing down to a new low near 33.49. However, note that the MACD failed to cross through the zero line and rolled back down. Therefore, it is not the indicator's fault that the market took one more dive before reaching the actual bottom.

The MACD was described in Chapter 4 as another indicator that shows the relationship between moving averages. It is the difference between a 26-period and a 12-period exponential moving average when you use your software vendor's default setup. The difference is calculated and then plotted in a histogram as a displacement from zero. Therefore, the data in the histogram are similar to the plotted difference between two moving averages under price drawn as a solid line. The MACD goes a step further by using a 9-period exponential moving average of the first average to form the "signal" (or "trigger") line, which is plotted on top of the MACD to show buy-sell opportunities.

The MACD was developed by Gerald Appel. It is used in the same way as the other oscillators that have been described so far. You should look for divergences between the indicator and the price data to detect oversold and overbought conditions. Three setups that you can look at are Appel's combinations 13–26–9 (you will see why Appel uses 13 and not 12 in a moment), 5–24–8, and 5–34–5. Regardless of the three periods you use, this indicator has the greatest lag or the slowest reaction to trend reversals. To help minimize this lag problem, Appel sets up two totally different MACD windows.

Appel's MACD Setup

Since most markets decline more rapidly than they rise, it is advisable to employ a more rapid combination (shorter-term moving average pairings) to track declining markets. I employ a 13-day, 26-day exponential average pairing to generate buy signals and a 19-day, 39-day pairing to generate sell signals. A 50-day moving average is employed to define a trend. If the average is rising sharply, indicating a strong uptrend, you would employ an even more rapid MACD pairing (6-day, 19-day) to generate buy signals and might delay selling until negative divergences appeared even if the signal line for the sell MACD was violated.

These comments are relevant to a strong bull market. A faster setup would be paired with the original setup for timing improvements in a larger-trending bear market. Therefore, when you set up two windows with MACD, the shorter or faster indicator setup is used to detect extremes in the shorter time horizon so that you can enter or add to existing positions within larger trends. Although one divergence in MACD may be sufficient, as this formula is slow, the Stochastic Oscillator often is paired with the MACD because it is a faster indicator by nature and should form two or three divergences with repeatedly lower volume with each divergence.

One's preference among indicators is entirely personal and depends on one's trading style. A common misunderstanding is that the Stochastic Oscillator or RSI can be used to confirm the MACD. *Do not make this error.* Together these indicators form a single timing signal, but they do not confirm one another because all three studies are various averages derived from price data. You need a non-correlated method to obtain confirmation. Confirmation simply means an increased probability that the expected outcome will occur. Therefore, non-correlated comparisons such as an Elliott Wave pattern with an MACD signal offers confirmation. A momentum signal would be non-correlated with a sentiment indicator or an indicator derived from volume.

Figure 9.2 shows a weekly chart for IBM with the Stochastic and RSI oscillators added. Moving averages are shown directly on top of the oscillators. Look for support and resistance when the oscillator tests the averages. One signal to monitor in particular when averages are used with either price or oscillators is a test that is made right at the crossover of your two averages, or when the oscillator turns right at the averages. The asterisks in Figure 9.2 help to clarify these important formations.

The indicators have very different appearances. They tell the same story, but in a slightly different manner. It comes down to personal preference; do not use both.

This chart provides an opportunity to clarify another use for moving averages. This is still part of the school of thought that says that prices can reveal everything, but you are going to go about it in a slightly different manner this time.

Both sides of Figure 9.3 show a monthly chart for IBM, allowing an important comparison of two different volatility band formulas. There is a difference between an envelope that uses two averages in which the bands are displayed with a fixed percentage above and below the mean value of price closes and the bands displayed in Figure 9.3. The thinking here is that when traders press a market into the band extremes, there is a high risk that market reversals will occur. Envelopes and volitility bands can be used in any time horizon.

The bands in Figure 9.3 are a little more sophisticated than fixed percentages. To understand the formula used to develop the bands shown on the left, you need to understand the concept of the standard deviation, a statistical measure of volatility that, once calculated, can be added to the moving average for the data. The bands in the left chart are Bollinger Bands, which are calculated in this manner. They plot

Figure 9.2 Weekly Chart for IBM with Stochastic and RSI Oscillators

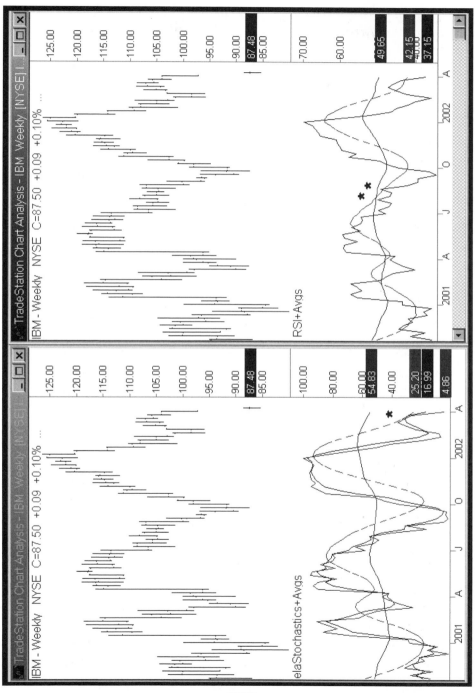

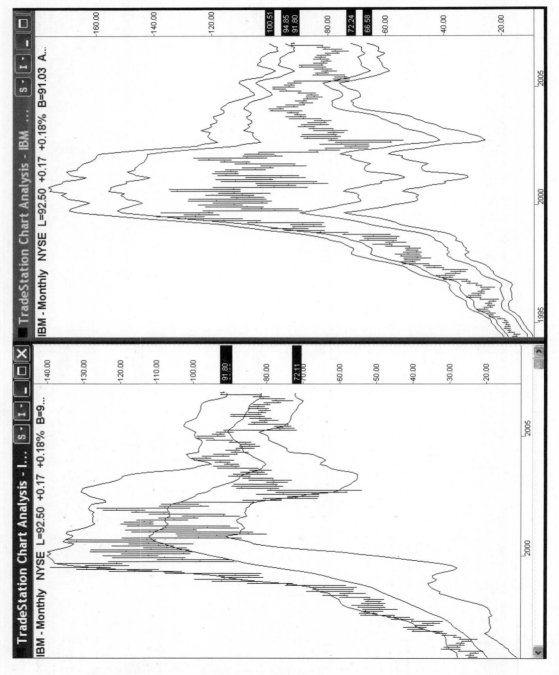

Figure 9.3 Monthly Chart for IBM

standard deviations above and below a moving average. The bands automatically adjust to changing market volatility. (These bands were developed by John Bollinger and became popular because he displayed them on FNN, which now is CNBC.)

One of the weaknesses of Bollinger Bands is demonstrated in this chart. In strong market moves, the price data stay outside the extreme ranges for some time. I tend to want to read bands as being maximum market displacements that precede an immediate reaction, and so I favor the formula displayed on the right side of Figure 9.3. When you are adding or subtracting to your preferred methods, it is important to test them side-by-side in a real-time environment. For many months these two methods were displayed side-by-side in different time horizons until I weeded one out. I never use the one on the left and use the one on the right only to read odd currency crosses. In an earlier example I suggested the use of an oscillator from just the spread between averages rather than a normalized indicator when the market was in a total meltdown. That application is called detrending.

The formula you use is a matter of personal preference. I use the bands on the right side of Figure 9.3 to see price failures during secondary tests; in other words, prices that touch the band once, react, then try to touch it a second time, and fail to reach it. This failure becomes the market timing signal to take action. A stall also works nicely. These are the only signals I look for within the bands.

The other use of bands is shown in the right-hand chart. IBM is in an extreme situation in terms of the price placement in the recent move. The price will not top, however, until it fails to reach the band. Thus, right now it is known that the price action will extend, and the pattern described will help with the market timing. The formula is in a format that can be used with any version of TradeStation (see Figure 9.4). You will need to work with your software vendor if you use a different system.

Both band formulas have the same characteristics in that they narrow significantly when markets become stable and quiet. This period of band narrowing often is followed by an explosive market move.

Study of Volume and Market Activity

Some investors believe that market breadth is the best way to determine market direction. This school of thought stresses the study of volume because these traders think that price alone is insufficient no matter what price-dependent approach one favors. The indicators and methods used by market breadth analysts track what is called market internals, such as volume and the number of advancing

Figure 9.4 Starc Band Formula

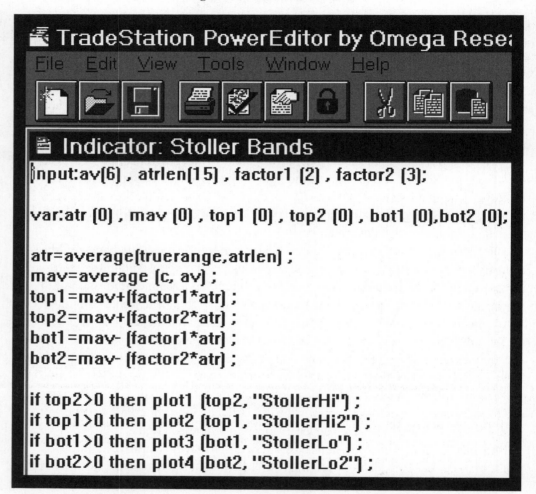

```
TradeStation PowerEditor by Omega Rese

File  Edit  View  Tools  Window  Help

Indicator: Stoller Bands

input:av(6) , atrlen(15) , factor1 (2) , factor2 (3);

var:atr (0) , mav (0) , top1 (0) , top2 (0) , bot1 (0),bot2 (0);

atr=average(truerange,atrlen) ;
mav=average (c, av) ;
top1=mav+(factor1*atr) ;
top2=mav+(factor2*atr) ;
bot1=mav- (factor1*atr) ;
bot2=mav- (factor2*atr) ;

if top2>0 then plot1 (top2, "StollerHi") ;
if top1>0 then plot2 (top1, "StollerHi2") ;
if bot1>0 then plot3 (bot1, "StollerLo") ;
if bot2>0 then plot4 (bot2, "StollerLo2") ;
```

shares versus the number of declining shares. Market breadth analysts generally are interested in stocks, and that is why nearly all these methods employ some comparison of stock activity.

An extremely popular indicator called the Advance/Decline Line is shown in Figure 9.5. The New York Stock Exchange Composite Index is displayed above the indicator. The advance/decline line is the difference between the number of stocks listed on the NYSE that advanced in price and the number that declined in price. Proponents of this school of thought do not use the actual price but use the relative

Figure 9.5   The Advance/Decline Line

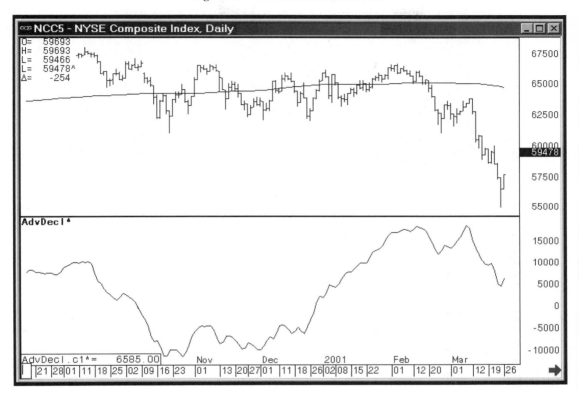

performance across the exchange as a bellwether. Other breadth indicators that have the same underlying premise are the Absolute Breadth Index, the Arms Index, the McClellan Oscillator, and the McClellan Summation Index.

Market breadth indicators are used to evaluate market strength. If there are more stocks with advancing prices than stocks with declining prices, this is a sign of internal market strength. Plotting an average rather than plotting the raw value alone usually smooths the absolute value.

Another popular market breadth indicator is the McClellan Oscillator, which was developed by Sherman and Marian McClellan. In a healthy bull market, a large number of stocks are making moderate upward advances in price. A weakening bull market is characterized by a small number of stocks making large advances in price, giving the false appearance that all is well. This type of divergence is viewed as a warning signal that an end could be near. A similar interpretation applies to market bottoms in which the market index continues to decline while fewer stocks are declining. Extreme readings in the McClellan Oscillator are viewed as high-risk trend reversal points.

The Arms Index is widely used for breadth analysis. To calculate the Arms Index, divide the number of stocks that advanced in price by the number of stocks that declined in price to determine the advance/decline ratio. Next, divide the volume of advancing stocks by the volume of declining stocks to determine the upside/downside ratio. Finally, divide the advance/decline ratio by the upside/downside ratio. If this is of interest to you, I suggest reading the books of Richard Arms, who is the originator of this indicator. (All breadth indicators experience slow market reactions at price extremes and can remain in those extreme conditions. I view them as analysis tools rather than market entry/exit trading signals.)

STUDY OF MARKET PARTICIPANTS

The third school of thought contains some very original methods favored by the market behavior analysts in the industry. In general, market psychology involves monitoring specific market participants and interpreting their actions as an indication of what prices will do next. Obtaining the data will require a little more work on your part, but the Internet is making everyone's life much easier, as charts can be viewed directly on the Web. Because some of the raw data are not easily available to the general public, few investors know how to read the Commitment of Traders.

Figure 9.6 shows a Microsoft Excel chart that I derived from Commitment of Traders data involving the activity of futures traders; it can be obtained from the exchange for a single week or purchased in historical files from various vendors. Every futures market has speculative buyers and sellers who never want to receive or deliver the underlying commodity. Some traders, known as hedgers, *do* want to complete the transaction and deliver or receive the commodity. Hedgers have different margin requirements than speculators and are required to report their open positions to the exchanges. As a result, there is a known reported number that reflects the activities of the commercial hedgers as opposed to those of the speculators.

The thinking is that the commercial traders have been correct more often than have the speculators. The chart in Figure 9.6 shows commercial traders' and speculators' activity in S&P 500 futures. In early 2000 the commercial traders held more short positions than they did at any other time in history. In contrast, the speculative public held the greatest number of net long positions within a 5-year

Figure 9.6   Excel Chart Derived from Commitment of Traders Data

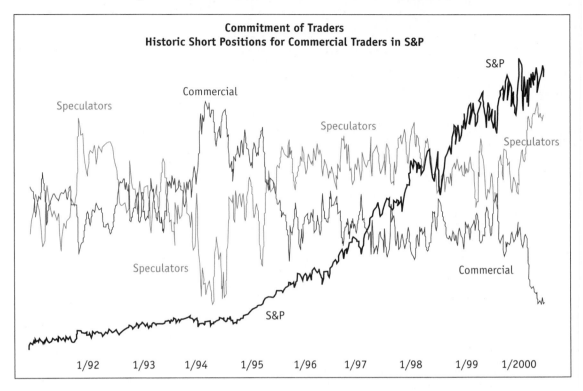

period. Although the commercial traders were early as usual, they correctly called the bigger market move, and the speculative public lost its bet big-time. That is why this information is used by stock traders.

Sentiment followers watch the activity of options traders. The put/call ratio (P/C ratio) is a market sentiment indicator that shows the relationship between the number of option puts and the number of option calls that are traded on the Chicago Board Options Exchange (CBOE).

A call gives an investor the right to purchase 100 shares of a stock at a predetermined price. Investors who purchase calls expect the price of the stock to rise in the coming months. Conversely, a put gives an investor the right to sell 100 shares of a stock at a preset price. Because investors who purchase calls expect the market to rise and investors who purchase puts expect the market to decline, the relationship between the number of puts and the number of calls illustrates the bullish versus bearish expectations of those investors.

Technical Analysis Demystified

Most of the volume in the option markets is generated by the speculative mass public. Therefore, as with the Commitment of Traders data, it is assumed that when the majority of speculators in the general public begin to favor one side of the market, the market will prove them wrong by moving in the opposite direction. The P/C ratio is a contrarian indicator; that means that the higher the P/C ratio is, the more bearish investors are on the market. Conversely, lower readings indicate high call volume and thus bullish expectations. Therefore, "excessive" levels warn investors that the market may have a trend change as a result of overextended sentiment.

Figure 9.7 shows a chart created by www.DecisionPoint.com. The top portion displays the S&P 100 Index. On the bottom is an indicator reflecting the put-to-call volume. The raw data are a little too wild and need to be smoothed. To solve this problem, one charts a simple moving average of the data rather than the raw data. DecisionPoint.com has used a 10-day moving average of the P/C ratio, which is very common.

Normally, the P/C ratio for the OEX Index is displayed as an inverse relationship to the S&P 100 price data. However, inverse relationships are hard to compare. If you look at the bottom right and the y axis labels in Figure 9.7, you will see that I have taken the indicator and turned it upside down. Use the tool Microsoft Paint,

Figure 9.7   10-Day Moving Average of Put/Call Ratios

which comes free with all Microsoft operating systems, to frame the section you want to turn upside down. After I have flipped the indicator, all my chart labels are upside down. Normally that does not cause a problem, as I just look at the visuals. However, for this book I also flipped the label on the bottom left and the months in the middle of the chart so that you could read them. That is why the arrows corresponding with what are now peaks are discontinuous.

Other sentiment ratios can be created from options trading. Figure 9.8, which also is from DecisionPoint.com, shows examples of CBOE P/C and equity P/C ratios. These are not inverse relationships, and the indicator labels show that the chart has not been altered from the way it was first presented on the Internet site.

The concepts behind market sentiment involving options will serve you well for other sentiment indicators you may wish to explore. As an example, the Member Short Ratio measures the short-selling activity of members of the New York Stock Exchange. Members trade on the floor of the exchange, and stocks that are sold short from the floor are viewed as the smart money, as opposed to the Public Short

Figure 9.8   CBOE Put/Call and Equity Put/Call Ratios

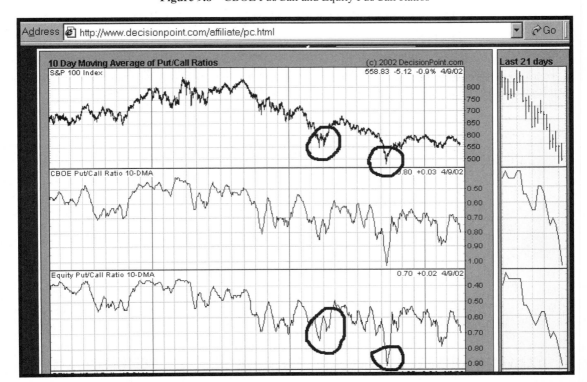

Ratio. Thus, a comparison is made between the activities of different participants in the market, just as was done in the Commitment of Traders chart (Figure 9.6). The source data may be different, but the concepts are the same.

As you develop your own system, be clear about which of these three groups you are studying. The key is to develop three non-correlated signals and watch for them to come together with one message to buy or sell.

Quiz for Chapter 9

1. Technical analysis is used by which two primary groups of traders?
   a. Investors and economists
   b. Fundamentalists and sentimentalists
   c. Systematic and intuitive traders
   d. Retail and institutional traders
   e. Geometry and sentiment traders

2. Technical indicators fall into which of the following four types of study groups?
   a. Short interest, short ratios, long interest, and long ratios
   b. Geometry, momentum, sentiment, and breadth
   c. Bar, candlestick, line, and point-and-figure
   d. Histograms, spreads, vectors, and direction
   e. Long, short, long to side, and short to side

3. Three non-correlated market analysis methods are:
   a. Stochastic Oscillator, RSI, momentum
   b. Stochastic Oscillator, MACD, detrended averages
   c. Trend, vectors, price channels
   d. RSI, retrograde time analysis, Elliott Wave
   e. Put/call ratios, ADXR, Michigan Consumer Sentiment Index

4. Back-testing an indicator with historical data from the 1990s:
   a. Is a method for curve fitting an indicator over a time period
   b. Provides a sufficient amount of history because it includes one bull market and one bear market cycle
   c. Gives false performance results and should not be used

d. B and C

     e. A, and is risky when volatility moves outside the original look-back window of time

5. Keltner Channels and Bollinger Bands are both:

     a. Measurements of price movement extremes

     b. Measurements of market sentiment extremes

     c. Measurements of market volatility

     d. Immediate directional signals when the extreme ranges are touched by prices

     e. Immediate signals to take profits or exit the market

6. When traders are said to be trading "in size," they are:

     a. Trading stocks in 1000-share blocks

     b. Trading futures in 10-block units

     c. Trading foreign exchange currencies in million-dollar multiples

     d. Trading the full sized NASDAQ futures rather than E-mini contracts

     e. Trading for a large fund

7. Which of the following can be said about momentum and sentiment indicators?

     a. They indicate when the majority of market participants will be caught in a bear or bull trap

     b. They cannot determine how far the market will move from a reversal

     c. They cannot warn investors when the market is at a high-risk pivot

     d. They can be used to develop a system of high probability without other non-correlated indicators

     e. They should never be charted for intraday price data

8. Relative opening and closing prices can be studied to:

     a. Determine market strength

     b. Determine market trend

     c. A and B

     d. Determine strength on market close

     e. Determine strength on market open

9. Which of the following is an example of a market breadth indicator?

     a. The number of stocks advancing today

     b. The Williams Oscillator

    c. The histogram within the MACD indicator

    d. The NYSE advance/decline line

    e. The OEX

10. Behaviorists develop formulas to do which of the following?

    a. Study the buying and selling patterns of mass crowds

    b. Study the buying and selling activity of retail versus institutional traders

    c. Study the buying and selling activity of the bearish crowd versus that of the bullish crowd

    d. Study the number of analysts with bearish newsletters versus analysts with bullish newsletters

    e. All of the above

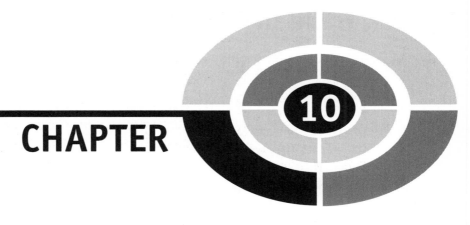

CHAPTER 10

Real-Time Trades Explained in Detail

Trading involves more than just learning the numerous methods described in this book. The ways to apply those methods are best learned by sitting beside a trader and watching over his or her shoulder. The problem here is that trading is done alone and no one wants the distraction of a student asking questions when he or she is on the front line doing battle. The next best option is for a trader to walk you through the thinking behind two trades to show the setup and how a decision was made.

A Stock Trade in the Energy Sector

Figure 10.1 shows a monthly chart for crude oil futures. However, in this example the trader is a stock trader only, and you need to examine ways to capitalize on a market you do not trade directly. As active futures trade up to a specific month and then roll over into a new month, the chart that is displayed is called a *perpetual chart*. There are ways to connect the different active futures contracts so that the historical data displays many years.

Figure 10.1 shows that oil has fallen sharply to a Fibonacci target level. The target level crosses the exact level where the simple moving average falls at $50. This target was realized in January 2007. How the target was derived is detailed in the book *Breakthroughs in Technical Analysis: New Thinking from the World's Top Minds*. I recommend that you read that book to see the release of original analyses collected from around the world.)

The oil market is of particular interest because it helps clarify a very important point: Never trade a stock or in a market without having a correlated market on which to lean. As an example, if you trade oil stocks, study energy futures. If you trade bank stocks, you need to have a market opinion about Treasury bonds and the 3-month eurodollar. It helps to have an opinion about Japanese Treasury bonds as well because they currently lead U.S. Treasury bonds. If you study oil, you will have an interest in sugar. Why? Sugar is used widely in South America to make ethanol, so the charts are correlated with oil. The trick here is knowing that they often have a slight difference in timing. When you find one market that leads another, you have a big edge.

Create a 3-month eurodollar chart with an overlay of inverted crude oil in a monthly time period. You will find that this inverse correlation maps very closely in each market. However, the 3-month eurodollar has a slight lead relative to the oil market. Therefore, when one turns, you have a warning about the other. This is called *intermarket analysis*. At the time the crude oil chart was captured in Figure 10.1, the 3-month eurodollar already had turned.

In Figure 10.1, the monthly oil chart shows a sharp decline to the target area. Not only is this a Fibonacci target level, the $50 area had geometry within the decline itself that pointed to the same area. That makes $50 a *confluence target zone*. When the market arrives at these critical areas, traders look to their indicators to see if they can provide permission to take action. In Figure 10.1, the relative strength index (RSI) is on a horizontal support zone near the point marked 2. If you study the RSI closely by tracking to the left, you will see that the momentum low at point 1 is on the same horizontal line. (A 1 has been placed under the price data that fit this RSI

Figure 10.1   Monthly Chart for Crude Oil Futures

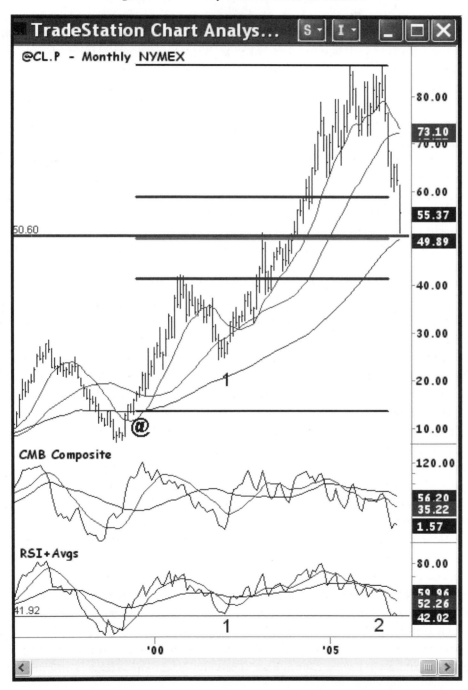

position.) It is clear that the larger rally began from this point. We have no divergence, but none is needed.

Consider the RSI positions at points 1 and 2. The RSI has fallen back to the same point that launched a large rally at point 1 near $25. However, oil has found support at $50 with the RSI at point 2. This shows a market that is finding support at a higher price, and the indicator can be said to be forming a positive reversal.

If you do not trade oil, how can you capitalize on a change coming in the futures market when you are in a stock position? You have to study energy sector charts. There are several sectors in which stocks are grouped together with companies that produce, service, or supply similar goods. Sometimes it is difficult to know which stock belongs to which group. Standard & Poor's has studied the revenue from each company and groups companies with similar revenue streams. In the case of oil stocks, there are a few stock groups to consider: oil drilling, oil equipment, oil and gas exploration, oil refining, oil well rig service companies, and international oil conglomerates.

When I looked at oil refining, the stocks SUN and ASH had conflicting charts. If there are conflicting trends within a group, I recommend looking elsewhere. As I scanned a page of stocks within a specific group, one sector stood out—the oil and gas exploration sector—because all the stocks in that sector had made corrections within incomplete rallies. Stocks that fall within this sector are EOG, APA, APC, and DVN. Because the stock sector gave a consistent message, I selected a stock that seemed to have the most compelling message to study further. The stock I selected was APC.

Figure 10.2 is a monthly chart for APC that shows that stock prices have declined to a target zone. The zone is marked with a horizontal band across the chart. Several Fibonacci retracement levels fell within the target band. All that remains in the chart is the band where they clustered together, which was put there for clarity. This allows your eye to track left. The support band falls just above the old price highs that formed in December 2000. It took the market 5 years to return to those levels. Old highs are extremely important, and APC is a stock that is testing its old historical highs. I also found a support zone at this area that was derived from the highs made in May 2006. If you study the price data alone, you can see that this is the second time this stock has declined to this particular support band. A double test of a key area of support is called a *double bottom directional signal*.

Technically the indicators are not overbought, and the composite index may show a hint of divergence compared with the RSI. The RSI has a history of

Figure 10.2   Monthly Chart for APC

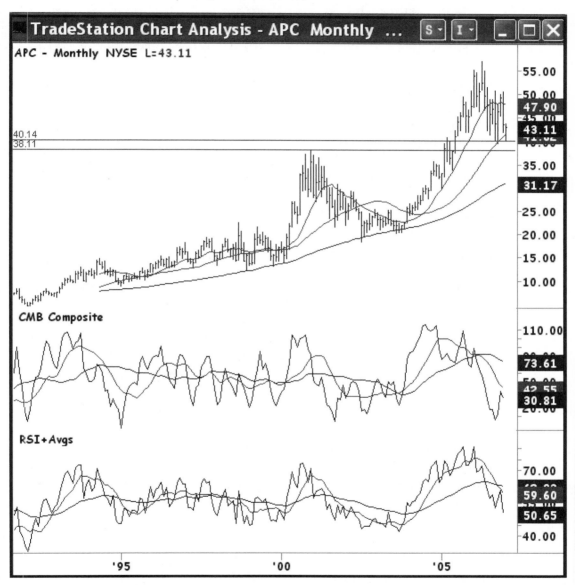

performing many tests of a horizontal level before the trend résumés. That provides a basis to be cautious because this may be a pivot point, but it could be short-lived, with another test coming after a bounce. The moving averages on price show a positive spread, but the indicators have averages as well, and they show that the spread is negative. (This is another reason to be cautious about longer-horizon charts.)

Figure 10.3 shows the double test of the support zone more distinctly. Both the composite and the RSI are oversold. The RSI, however, is forming its third attempt to bottom at the same horizontal level. That is a strong permission signal to consider buying this stock with stops just under the support zone. Both the weekly and the monthly momentum indicators are in agreement. This adds weight to the signal, and you will find that the weekly and monthly charts do not always agree. When the weekly chart is oversold and the monthly chart is overbought, the weekly chart will move up, and then, when the two are in agreement, a larger decline can develop. In a market that is forming a bottom, the weekly chart can be overbought but the monthly chart can be oversold. The weekly chart may be warning that another leg down is needed before a true bottom is in place. It is important to pay attention to the conflicts or agreements within the monthly and weekly charts. When I studied the daily chart, it too was trying to form a bottom.

If you did all your homework on the longer-horizon charts the night before, you would wait until the market open the next day. But in APC there was a very interesting market open. Figure 10.4 shows an intra-day chart for APC. This is a 22-minute chart. Recall from earlier chapters that a ratio of 4:1 is suggested for viewing charts. In stocks I find that an 88-minute chart is of greater value than a 60-minute chart. That means that I need a 22-minute chart for comparison. (You do not want to be confined to a vendor that gives you only a fixed menu of time periods. If you are a longer-horizon trader, you still need intra-day data. You have to be able to see the market in detail, not just the big picture.)

The market open in APC was interesting because it had a gap up open from the previous day. Figure 10.4 captured 11 bars after the open in question. The reason for the delay is that we were buying aggressively. The homework had been done, and now the market was presenting us with a gap up open. That is very significant because experienced traders know that a gap up open near a potential bottom is a breakaway gap and that the market should not—cannot—move down to fill the gap fully if the bottom is in place. Therefore, we scrambled to buy with tight stops under the gap. Within the first hour after the open, a small pullback followed to just the moving averages shown in this chart. That also showed strength, and then another wave up developed into a new high for the day that you can see in the more recent bars. (If you are a short- or long-horizon trader, you need to see this type of information. No one should be without intra-day data.)

The initial price target is only to 43.50, but with stops so close to the entry, it provides a win/loss ratio of 3-to-1. You do not want to step into a trade for less than

Figure 10.3   A Double Test of the Support Zone

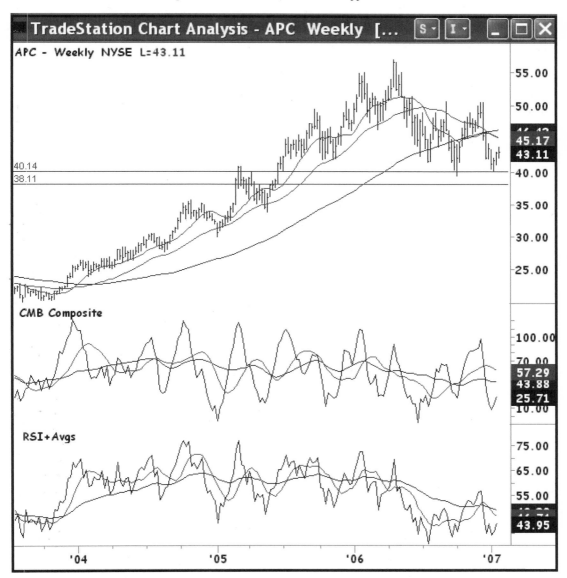

that. It makes no sense to risk a dollar to make two or, worse, risk a dollar to make a dollar. The amount you should risk should be a percentage of the total trading capital. Do not exceed 3 percent of your capital on the basis of the position of your stop versus your entry point. You will be using more than 3 percent of your capital

Figure 10.4   Intra-day Chart for APC

but will have at risk only 3 percent. If you are wrong, the total capital is reduced to calculate the next percentage. If you have a 3-to-1 win/loss ratio, you would be risking 3 percent and have a potential gain of 9 percent. You can see that the timing of a trade is very important because good timing allows a larger position with the same risk exposure. This is called *leverage*.

The energy sector can be very volatile and risky. You may want to reduce your risk further by trading two stocks in the same sector. If you trade two stocks in the same sector, split the risk by exposing only 1.5 percent of your capital in each position.

Figure 10.5 is a weekly chart for SLB, a stock in the same energy sector as APC. The weekly chart is also bullish. The composite index is diverging with the RSI. The RSI is making a double bottom as the composite establishes a rising trend line in the oscillator. The weekly data bounced off the moving average on the price data.

Figure 10.5   Weekly Chart for SLB

Figure 10.6   Chart Analysis for SLB

A method we have mentioned is called the Elliott Wave Principle. This is a method of reading patterned sentiment within the swings of price data. From the market high to the decline into the moving average, we have a completed corrective pattern. (This is something you can look into another time, but it made it easier for me to know that the larger rally was incomplete.) A non-correlated method always helps to add confidence and probability, and so we spread the risk and bought this stock as well. Our price target was back to the $70 range, and so this would offer a longer-horizon position. If we had been unsure about APC, we would have unwound it at the first target and considered this a risk reduction on the primary trade in SLB.

You can see that learning how to read a chart does not make a person a trader. The implementation and risk assessment require another level of expertise. When you begin to trade, risk management is of critical importance, as it will buy you the time to gain experience.

You can check your own computers to see how the SLB trade turned out. If we reached $70, we would reevaluate after taking at least half the position off to bank some of the profits. If a pullback warranted a full position again, we might carry 150 percent relative to the first leg up in the trade. But the entry would have to be under the exit and the stop placement could risk more than 1.5 percent on the basis of the first entry calculations.

In the same market open in which we discussed APC, it can be seen in Figure 10.6 that SLB also had a gap up open. Now there are two stocks in the same sector showing strength. This would add to one's confidence in the trade but should not change the amount a trader is willing to risk.

A Large Cap Stock Trade in the S&P 500 Index

On February 27, 2007, the Dow Jones Industrial Average (DJIA) fell 500 points in a single trading session. The news media and many American traders were surprised at that development because they felt that it was a reaction to China's recommendation that capital gains taxes be applied to that country's parabolic rallying stock markets. The chart shown in Figure 10.7 was captured in a real-time context. The fall in the DJIA was not a surprise to more advanced analysts of global stock indexes.

The three-day chart of the DJIA in Figure 10.7 shows that moving averages have narrowed with a negative spread on the momentum oscillator called the composite index (the heavy black line). The composite index momentum highs were getting lower and lower as the price tried to sustain the rally into new highs. This is classic bearish divergence that warns that a market has run out of steam.

Figure 10.7   Three-Day Bar Chart for the Dow Jones Industrial Average

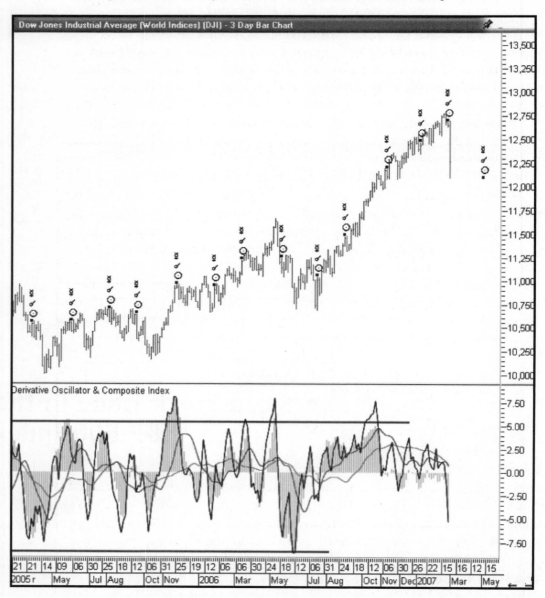

Behind the composite index there is a histogram. It is a different formula called the derivative oscillator. (Information about this oscillator can be found in my book *Technical Analysis for the Trading Professional*.) Throughout the first 8 weeks in

2007 the derivative oscillator was below zero. Here it shows only that the DJIA was very vulnerable to a sharp setback.

Figure 10.8 shows the Fibonacci retracement calculations described in detail in Chapter 3. The first area where two Fibonacci projections overlap, which is called the *confluence zone*, is exactly where the market fell. When you check your own charts, you'll see the market stayed that low and bounced toward the minor support level

Figure 10.8   Fibonacci Retracement Calculations for the Dow Jones Industrial Average

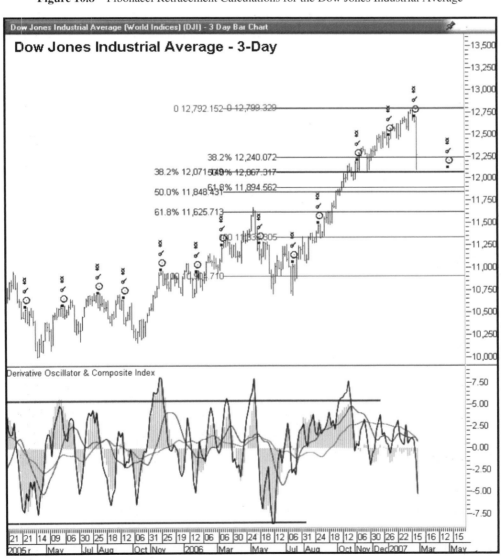

drawn above this confluent target zone. The indicator shows that this market often needs a more complex bottom, and the composite index was not at a level that could sustain a longer-term bottom. Therefore, after a bounce into overhead resistance, another leg down to the lower support zone developed. This chart shows only the Fibonacci retracements. We also calculated Gann target levels and found that 11,909 actually marked the top of the support zone in this chart at 11,848–11,894. The DJIA used the top of the zone as the place to bottom.

We knew a week before that the DJIA was at a very high risk pivot. We also knew this decline would be fully retraced. In this chart you can see an astrological cycle that has been mapped on the data. Because this is a three-day chart, the date bullets leave little squiggle room to see if they are respected by the market. (Chapter 6 discussed cycles, and you will see in this chart how they are applied.) This cycle is not a fixed-period interval but simply was used in a mathematical manner without any thought given to astrological interpretation. It is necessary only to be aware when the cycle occurs, and the computer drops a bullet on the day. A future bullet can be seen to the far right marking another time target.

The fundamentalists all blamed China for upsetting the global party. However, this type of event is not altogether surprising if one has any chart awareness of overseas markets.

Figure 10.9 provides a weekly view of the Shenzhen Composite Index, China's answer to the DJIA. (Anyone can get price data to track from the Internet. You can order end-of-day data from a company called CSI DATA. The product, which is called Unfair Advantage, is very inexpensive to lease for a year. Through this vendor you can track any global market you want to see.)

In the Shenzhen Composite, one can see a set of numbers marking specific swings. (These notations are Elliott Waves.) Over the price high, you will see two astrological bullets that overlap. This is the same idea as Fibonacci targets that overlap to form a major target. This was a confluent time target, and the index began its global meltdown from this precise spot. The technical indicator also is trying to diverge, but note that the averages on the indicator remain positive. That means that the coming decline can be ugly but will be retraced fully. Knowing that China can recover fully before a larger decline indicates that the decline in the DJIA will also attempt a rally from this deep breakdown. Once the DJIA made the second leg down toward 11,909, we wanted to buy a few stocks. (That is where a trader can look at how to capitalize on this information when most traders are still in a panic.)

The first thing you want to know is whether other American indexes concur with your opinion. You are not going to buy on the basis of the DJIA chart alone.

Figure 10.9 China's Shenzhen Composite Index (Weekly)

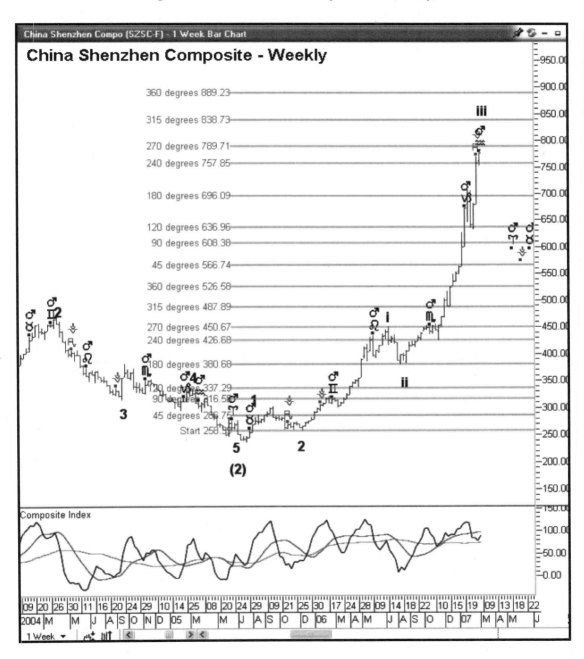

Figure 10.10 shows a chart for NASDAQ futures. It more clearly demonstrates the sharp hard break that found support at a major confluence target zone obtained from Fibonacci retracement analysis. The market bounced and failed under a resistance area. Prices then fell to a confluence zone marking support under the most recent bar on the far right. Here the NASDAQ is tracking the same scenario as the DJIA and holding its own levels of support. *There is confirmation.*

As we reviewed stock sectors, we found a stock that clearly had an incomplete rally and was defining a strong trend before all the excitement about China hit the wires.

Figure 10.10   NASDAQ Futures

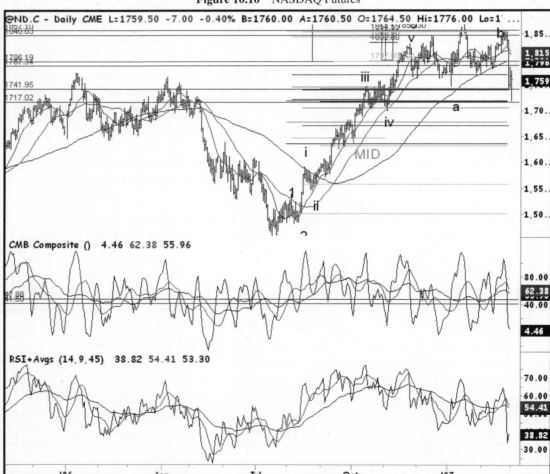

Goodyear Tire (GT) is shown in a weekly view in Figure 10.11. We needed a stock that was not in the energy group because we needed to diversify. We found six we liked, and GT was at the top of the list. Why? GT can be said to provide several geometric clues. A measurement taken from the 2006 price lows into 22.35 marks a halfway point for the unfolding of the rally. The Fibonacci tool is used to take a measured move to project an equality swing up to define the target price. It targets 35, with a more conservative target near 31.

Most people make the projected swing up from a price retracement. We preferred to take profits ahead of the crowd and avoid a stampede to bank profits. Therefore, we started the swing projection from an imaginary midpoint that fell in the middle of the strongest swing upward within the rally. The momentum indicators in the weekly chart looked dreadful, but the daily chart was a compelling buy.

It is clear that the American markets are at a bottom and that sentiment has turned from bearish to panic. You can see that the monthly chart remains a buy. One of the time periods is out of sync, as you can see in Figure 10.11. That necessitates taking a smaller position because the probability of an immediate rally is not as strong as it is when all three time horizons agree. GT price and RSI are at extreme highs, but they are at new highs. The indicator will decline in a sideways or falling fashion, but it then will produce a strong move up to challenge the amplitude of the old momentum high extremes behind the oscillator position that now is making new highs. The averages also show an extremely positive spread. There is no question that this stock has room to produce further gains in the bigger picture.

The thing to consider now is the mathematics behind the risk exposure. You can see that the midpoint line falls at 22.35. You would not want to hold the position if GT fell below this line. Therefore, your line in the sand for a stop is just under this level. The stock is trading at 24.17. You have a conservative target at 31.50. You are risking about a dollar to make nearly 6. You want to buy, but your homework is not complete until you study a shorter time frame.

The daily data in Figure 10.12 show that GT has declined to major support at 24. The composite index is forming its third divergence signal to RSI. You then go back to look at price more closely in the daily chart and see that a directional signal is present. There is a double bottom where the data have tested the $24 support line two times. In the 15-minute chart (these screens were captured for you as we entered the trade in a real-time scenario), the composite again is diverging with the RSI. Price has a completed Elliott Wave pattern for corrections that is called a *zigzag decline*.

Figure 10.11   Weekly Chart for Goodyear Tire

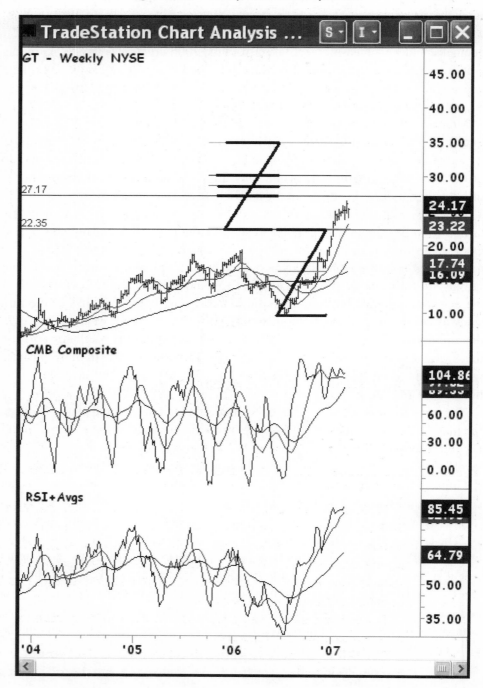

Figure 10.12   Major Support for Goodyear Tire (GT)

What is not in the chart is the knowledge that the DJIA, the NASDAQ, and the S&P are all on a time target turn date. Time targets were introduced in the chapter discussing cycles. You have seen examples in prior charts. Therefore, you consider all the evidence with the knowledge that the indexes cannot break their major support zones and GT cannot be permitted to make a new low. You are at the low, so enter the market with tight stops.

Some time passed, and we recorded the short intraday chart to show the action off the price lows (see Figure 10.13).

The GT stock moved up immediately when the DJIA started to stabilize. In a short-horizon trade, you would take some profit into the first target zone and then

Figure 10.13 Action Off the Price Lows for Goodyear Tire

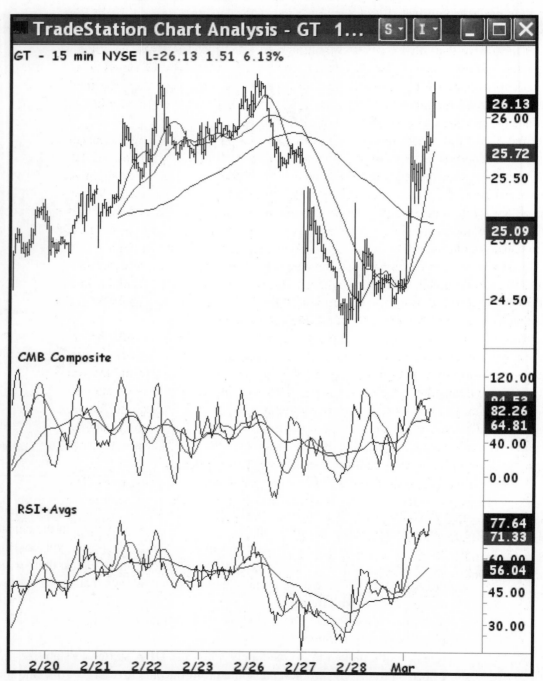

add on a pullback that probably would test the averages in this chart. A longer-horizon trader would just sit tight and wait to see the outcome. We did both: We took 40 percent of the position off *and* added 65 percent at a slightly lower level. That means we then held a position of 125 percent of our usual size. Our capital exposure did not exceed 3 percent of the account size, and because of the issues in the weekly chart, we had to scale back to 2 percent capital risk. Thus, the final position was a little more than 2 percent risk, but we had banked a small profit to reduce the risk back to 2 percent with greater leverage.

Figure 10.14 is a new monthly chart that shows GT at 32.10. The Fibonacci retracement derived in this time horizon showed a major confluence zone at 32.10, slightly higher than the target derived from the shorter-horizon target. We took most of the profit off the table with a market order at the 31.10 level. (It was under the target, as we did not need perfection.) The balance was unwound, and this chart captures the trade completely. It probably will stall here and then run to the next level near 40, but the DJIA and global markets once again are looking risky.

Therefore, we ran to the bank and left the stock for someone else to figure out. The indicators in this chart have run to new highs, and it warns that further extensions upward will develop. But it is preferable to start the process all over again from a pullback as the weekly and daily charts are now both overbought.

These two trading examples cover many key elements for you to consider before entering an order. Do you have confirmation in other stocks in the sector? Do you have permission from your indicators at a key support or resistance level? Do you know where the market is going and where it should not trade before you establish the trade? Can you find evidence to support your opinion in other markets that are correlated? Can you establish a position risking less than 3 percent of your total capital? Do you have a minimum 3-to-1 win-to-loss ratio? It is not enough just to have a market opinion about the single stock chart before you.

I wish you market success and the discipline to follow your trading rules. The markets test every trader, and there is always more to learn. However, before we part, I would like to leave you with a few thoughts about why many traders lose before they learn how to win in the markets. Maybe you can avoid some of the common pitfalls. There is much more to trading than just focusing on the development of your technical charting skills. Successful traders understand themselves and how human nature can influence how we make decisions.

Figure 10.14   Monthly Chart for Goodyear Tire

Why You Win or Lose

Human Nature Gets In the Way

Do you have a dream? Do you know why you would like to be a successful trader? My dream was to own a horse farm and awake each morning with a smile knowing my four-legged friends were waiting for me to feed them breakfast. The journey has taken me to the top of the World Trade Tower in New York City, to the bright lights of the world's largest financial cities. I have no regrets, but 9/11 became my wake-up call. The next thing on my to-do list was to start living my life. Every day is precious and I had to stop putting my personal goals to the side in favor of professional activities. You need a dream as it's not about the accumulation of more and better stuff.

Trading is about testing one's character rather than testing one's skill. I'll demonstrate for you.

We do not win or lose based on what we know alone, the net outcome rests on human psychology. Certain psychological traits that we all have are barriers to success. The questions in Chapter 8 were all True or False patterns. But every question had a "True" answer. I was messing with your mind to illustrate a point. How many questions did you read before you began to think, "this can't possibly be a 'True' answer again"? Did you begin to doubt your answer early or late in the series? Did you change your answers because the pattern messed with your mind? Why should the prior answer influence the correct answer for the next question? Why does a prior trade impact our actions for the next trade with the same setup? Why, when you had a profit on a certain stock did you not sell it? Why did you stand by and see a profit reduced as prices went lower and lower without ever offering to sell?

Living in horse country might make one think I would never see market psychology in action again unless I'm sitting in front of my computer. However, I watched with wonder as an old hunter demonstrated the art of catching turkeys on a fall day. You will see as the story unfolds that the hunter was demonstrating the human psychology that traders struggle with daily. He had a turkey trap—a crude contraption consisting of a big box with a door hinged at the top. This door was kept open by a prop to which was tied a piece of twine leading back a hundred feet or more to the operator. A thin trail of corn scattered along a path lured turkeys to the box. Once inside they found an even more plentiful supply of corn. When enough turkeys had wandered inside, the plan was to jerk away the prop and let the door fall shut.

The old man arrived at his box to see a dozen turkeys in his box. Then, one must have heard our arrival because it strode out cautiously to see what was brewing outside the corn feast.

"Gosh, I wish I had pulled the string when all twelve were there," said the old man. "I'll wait a minute and maybe the other one will go back to join the others."

But while he waited for the twelfth turkey to return, two more walked out on him.

"I should have been satisfied with eleven," he said. "Just as soon as I get one more back I'll pull the string."

But then three more turkeys walked out. Still the man waited. Having once had twelve in his trap he clearly disliked having to go home with less than eight now. He couldn't give up the idea that some of the original number would return. When finally only one was left in the trap, he said:

"I'll wait until he walks out or another walks in, and then I'll quit. If another walks in I'll feel ahead, but one turkey is hardly worth all the effort."

He walked away without any turkeys. True story and it fits all traders at some point in the early stages of their career, since most traders do not know when to jerk the string and close the trap. There are tools within this book to help you recognize when the trap should be closed and precise ways to know when to save the entire empty trap and run for the hills. The markets test us in so many ways and our human nature gets in the way all the time.

Develop the Confidence to be Independent from Everyone

One common fault within the retail market, which is the label used for the small private trader or investor, is that they are unsure of themselves so they assume everyone else around them must have a better opinion. You know the profile: a neighbor who passes along a tip, a relative who states their company's earnings report is about to be a surprise when announced tomorrow, the local wheeler-dealer who blurts a tip at the local coffeehouse in the early morning shuffle. Early in my own career I used to record my first broker's recommendations. Months later I confirmed my suspicions that most of what I heard him recommend was dead wrong. Why?

Don't Fight a Strong Trend

People are inclined to buy poor stocks because they feel good buying a lot of a low-priced stock. People also have no concept of timing within a trend. Oversold can get considerably more oversold and vice versa. After extensive study about technical indicators they go with their gut feeling that it is time this stock *should* go up, and they ignore the tools they have studied hard to learn. The loss is not from the indicators, but from the psychological handicap they place on themselves. It is no different than thinking you just answered seven questions that where "True," surely this next one will be "False." But the previous seven questions offered an established trend. Why buck the trend for the sake of a change?

Experience Can Make Trading Harder

Many novice traders have early success and then wonder why they give it all back and then some to the markets. Generally, novice traders have no idea how to limit their losses, but the greatest factor is that they have no experience of just how bad it feels to lose. You are always under fire when you trade and you will inevitably take a few bullets. But if you don't have a bullet proof vest to manage the loss, the psychological damage turns to self-doubt and fear to pull the trigger. It gets much harder to dig yourself out of a financial hole. It could be a greater challenge to your ego than anything you might have faced before in your life. If you tie your personal self-worth to your trading success it will be even harder. The number of negative experiences you have will grow over time, then the battle scars fresh in your memory will begin to play tricks on your mind and you will become more cautious. Wiser, yes. But you will know how low your emotions can go if you make a mistake and experience the pain that follows a loss. The only way to survive is to have strict money management rules. The purpose of these rules is not only to save your bank roll, but also to save you from psychological damage, which is much harder to repair.

Mentally Unbalanced by Only Buying Stock and Never Selling Short

Many stock traders are too mentally unbalanced to trade a market from both sides. I cannot tell you the number of retail people I've had discussions with who think all they can do with a stock account is buy stock. Excuse me, you can sell stock short as well! It doesn't take a special account other than a normal margin account. The same account that accepts buy orders will accept sell short orders. You need to know how to enter all orders.

When novice traders want to buy a stock, they think they are buying an asset that will undoubtedly appreciate. They hold the position for a couple of days, hours, or a few weeks. This thinking is hogwash. You are buying a number and want the number to go higher. Period. It will go up if other people think as you do. It's a number. Get over it. Therefore you can sell the number expecting it to go down to make a profit. It has nothing to do with ethics or selling against your country or whatever. Erase all these psychological handicaps. Buy it if you think the number will go up, sell if you think it is going down. As a stockowner you don't own squat because the senior debit bondholders have all the rights over a stock owner anyway. So think of it as a number until you can buy 5 percent of the total outstanding shares for the company. Until then, fundamentals just fuel the greed and fear factor behind the numbers. By using technical charts you are already measuring the fear and greed sentiment before the reports ever come out.

Lack of Knowledge About Order Types and Execution

The types of orders are *market orders, limit orders, sell stop order, buy stop order*, and simple *"buy and sell"* to exit a long position or *"sell short and buy to cover"* for a short position. If you do not know what it is to sell stock short, you should not be trading anything! You are psychologically chained to buy everything. You cannot look for opportunities in stocks falling versus rising. Your portfolio cannot carry positions on both sides of the market. If a housing stock like HOV is in a nosedive, you should be *short*. If telephone stocks are in a rally you should be *long*. You become long by having bought the stock. You become short by *selling short*. When you want out of your long position to bank the profit at a higher number, you sell the stock. To bank a profit when you are short you enter an order to *buy-to-cover* at a price lower than what you sold it. Having both long and short positions established helps to offset the risk of the other and you are mentally balanced in your trading decisions. What is short selling you ask? Good! Look up "short selling" on the Internet before you read on. One site to try is http://www.investopedia.com/university/shortselling/shortselling1.asp.

If your brokerage firm makes it hard for you to enter these orders by not displaying a sell short order in their selection of order types, move your account to a firm that has it ready to go. If you have a margin account you have the ability to sell stock short now. Basically the broker is loaning you stock to sell when you don't own it. Since you are borrowing stock on margin to sell stock that is not yours, eventually you will have to return it to the broker by buying it back to cover the short position. In essence you borrowed stock and returned it. Therefore you want the stock to cost less when you return the borrowed shares.

Can your brokerage firm accept a sell stop at the *same time* you establish the position? If not, move your account. The risk is all on your shoulders, not the brokerage firm's if you do not know the order types. They will make money with you coming and going, whether you win or lose. Period. So it is important to do your homework. There is nothing special about a short sale, but so many people have no idea they can buy *and* sell any stock.

The purpose of a stop order is to limit a loss or protect a profit. Many people lose a lot of money because they do not understand the orders available to them. For example, in a sell stop order, the trader may have purchased one crude oil contract at $74. He is willing to accept a loss of about 15 points, but he doesn't want to take a loss much beyond that amount, so he will instruct the brokerage firm to execute a sell stop at $73.85. When the market trades at or through $73.85 the contract is sold *at-the-market* and he may get a different price like $73.82. The fill is often at a price lower than the stop because the order becomes a market order for execution. This is all normal, but let's say OPEC makes an announcement that they intend to flood the oil market and suddenly prices plummet. You get filled at 68.10 or wherever the floor was able to fill your market order, but at least you are filled and out of the trade. Traders who state they want $73.85 by using a limit order are still holding the contract if the market gapped down over their limit at $73.85. The same traders are still in the position if a fast market slides through $73.85 preventing a fill at their price.

While you should always enter protective buy or sell stops, do you understand a "stop *limit* order" is the most deadly order to use? A *sell stop* is an order to sell if the market touches or exceeds the sell level you identify. The order to sell automatically becomes a market order to sell at any price. If you use a sell stop limit order and define an exact price the order has to be filled at your defined price. You will discover one day that this order cannot be filled at your level and you are losing more money with every tick the market moves against you. If the market gaps and never trades at your limit price, you are still in the position, taking a loss down to a price of zero.

If you are positioned *short* use a *buy stop* over the market entry price. If you entered a restriction by using a *buy limit stop* when a stock has a takeover announcement, you might find the stock is $20 over your stop (you expected the stock to fall). There is nothing you can do until you enter a market order, in this case, *buy-to-cover*. If they cannot execute your order at your *exact limit level* the position going sour has no way to cut its losses. This is an unwise order to use. I've introduced several different order types in the last few paragraphs. A quick illustration may help you keep these different orders clear.

IBM trades at $100. You buy 1 share IBM *at-the-market*. You have established a *long* position and want the market to go up. The *sell stop* is entered at the same time as the purchase. Use a *sell stop* at $97 as an example. When the market hits $97 or lower the order goes in to sell 1 share of IBM *at-the-market*. The order is filled and you are now *flat*. You have no position because selling 1 share offsets or covers the original purchase of IBM. Let us say you win and IBM trades at $107. You enter the order OCO, meaning one cancels the other. You sell one share of IBM *at-the-market* and cancel the sell stop at $97 at the same time. The fill is $106.82. You have a profit of $6.82 on the one share of IBM and your account is flat. *Flat* means you have no open position in your account or risk exposure to the market.

IBM trades at $100. You sell short 1 share of IBM. You have established a short position and want the market to go down. At the same time you enter a *buy stop* over your entry price at $103. If the market hits $103 or higher your buy stop becomes a market order to buy at-the-market and you may get a fill like $103.12. You lost $3.12 on your short position because it costs you more to return the stock you borrowed from the broker initially for $100. It also cost you a little to borrow the stock in the first place because you borrowed on margin.

Let's say you win and IBM falls to $93. You enter the order *buy-to-cover* 1 share of IBM at-the-market. You could get a fill of $93.10. You have a profit of $6.90. It is a profit because you sold 1 share of *borrowed* IBM stock at $100 and it only cost you $93.10 to return it to your broker. You keep the profit difference. Done? No! You forgot the stop was still being worked at $103. So you could have used an OCO order to cover both or cancel the stop. If you forget to cover your stop and you used a *GTC*, or Good 'til Canceled designation, you will end up owning 1 share of IBM without realizing it. An order that states *One Cancels the Other* (OCO), should be easily handled by your brokerage firm. TradeStation just asks the question: Do you want your stop canceled when you exit this position? They then know to use OCO regardless of whether you know about that particular type of order or not.

The use of *MIT* or Market-If-Touched orders is an ill-advised order if the reward is greater than three or four times the amount being risked. You do not want to trade a win-to-loss ratio less than 3:1 so don't try to squeeze into the trade at a price level that marks perfection. Just buy the darn thing (or short it) at-the-market and stop nano-ticking the entry. Sometimes it takes months for new traders to discover they don't get extra credit if they bought or sold the lowest or highest tick. No one cares. If you are trying to enter positions while you are doing something else away from the computer, you are not a trader. Price alone is not a reason to enter unless you have permission from your indicators. If you are not at the screen, how do you know the setup fits the strategy you considered for a specific price?

There are other orders such as *opening orders* and *closing orders* that direct the brokerage firm to execute within a time period. There are also *not held orders*, and *fill or kill orders*. Forget them and sit at the screen if you intend to trade.

Poor Understanding About Market Leverage and Account Margins

Do you understand leverage and margin? Margin is like taking out a mortgage on your home. The difference is you have to ante up more money if the bank thinks you are putting them at more risk than when you first borrowed the money to buy or short stock. In a mortgage, you don't have to give the bank more collateral because the value of the housing market is imploding. Mind you, you may have to pay them to get out of the mortgage contract when you sell if the value has fallen below the mortgage on the home. That's why no money down home purchases are risky. But many traders overlook these factors and do not understand the differences between futures, stock, and options margin and leverage calculations. Futures require you to put up about 5 percent of the value of the underlying contract. Great. At least at first glance it looks great. But you will go down 95 percent faster if you are standing on the wrong side of the teeter-totter. Most novice futures traders have no idea how leverage works against them. They know it goes up faster when they are right and do not understand what happens when they are on the wrong side of a market move until they are wiped out.

Lack of Knowledge About the Market Being Traded

How many people have dabbled in mini-futures contracts thinking they were reducing their risk by trading these half contract sizes in the NASDAQ or S&P? They think they have an idea of the risk they have exposed themselves to by entering a stop order. We just covered how stop orders are filled at-the-market." But then the futures trader learns a new phrase: *limit down*. That means we don't care how deep you are in debt right now, there is *no market* and it has just closed! It can happen at any hour the market hits the limit down breaker defined by an exchange. Some markets have limit up criteria as well. The next day the breaker is reset by the exchange and the limit could be even wider. If there are no buyers on the second day, the market continues to have you trapped in a losing position every day with no way for you to let go of the falling anchor costing you unlimited losses.

Using Stops Too Close to the Entry Level and Ignorance of the Daily Price Range

In the oil contract example I used a sell stop under the market at $73.85 for a position bought at $74. Do you realize there is something called a daily range? If you place a stop in the market it could be too close to the trading price and average daily range. The floor can hit your price just for being in the wrong place at the wrong time and then return the market right back to the higher price. It is called a gift to the house. Want to make another gift by placing a stop too close again? Go ahead, because no regulators on the floor will stop you. It is permitted because it is in the range of normal fluctuations. Do you know what the spread is for the stock or future contract you are looking at in a fast market condition or thin condition? None of this has anything to do with the technical indicators on your screen, but it has everything to do with knowing more about what it means to execute an order wisely and manage the risk.

Trading Markets with Insufficient Volume or Liquidity

If you are in a market that is very thin, which is a market with light or low volume and wide spreads between the bid and ask prices, I have to ask, *why are you trading it?* Do you understand what a bid and ask spread is telling you about a market? If you do not you need to monitor just a couple stocks and observe what happens when the spreads narrow and widen. The bid is the price someone is willing to pay for something and the asking price is what someone is willing to sell it to you. When you have a market maker on the floor, they have to try to step in the middle to narrow the spreads. I am using a lot of terms here and I suggest you look up every one of these phrases to learn how orders are executed and how markets function. We call this order flow. If it is electronic, how does an order get filled? If you only have access electronically, how will you stop a loss if the Internet shuts down? This knowledge makes the difference between a winner and a market loser.

While we have covered several ways to sabotage your best intentions to excel as a trader, human character will haunt you the rest of your days until you become a conscientious, competent student of market psychology.

Recognize Human Psychology Works Against a Trader

It takes tremendous discipline to trade knowingly against the natural tendencies that all humans share. The example of the hunter and his trap filled with turkeys is a prime example. But the line is thin between trapping a turkey and being the turkey when trading markets is concerned. Nearly everyone commits the same blunders at some point. The blunders are so widely shared that they can be considered normal crowd behavior of traders.

One of the challenges a trader faces is balancing personal pride and vanity. This could be one of the hardest challenges. Protecting our pride is one reason that leads us to take small profits, but have large losses. Even a tenth of a point profit is acceptable, because small as it is, you have nevertheless beaten the game. But a fractional loss hurts your pride, and instead of accepting this small loss after a stock begins to look sour, you say you'll wait to get out even. To take a loss is a confession that your original judgment was wrong and that is a hard thing for a fragile ego to admit. Unconsciously, you may say, "I'm going to make that loss up!" Then a $100 loss turns into a $1000 loss as you are chasing the prior trade and not the current one before you.

It is vanity that makes people buy more of the same stock in which they took a loss. Wall Street calls it *dollar-cost-averaging*. A professional will call it adding to a losing position. This is a bad investment in any language. The weaker a stock becomes, the more attractive it looks to some inexperienced traders. Heck, if you loved it at $56, you're going to be ecstatic about it at $10. Take the emotion out. It is just a number moving up or down. If you want to average or pyramid, average upward, not downward against yourself.

Next to vanity eating away our good judgment stands greed. You have learned a price projection method to use. Stick with your plan. If the market reaches your price target, get out. If you get to your target and think, "Gee, now I'll just hang around for the next target," you will lose. Avoid having to tell yourself, "Oh, if I had only sold when (insert trigger event here)!" We all have our share of greed and it takes tremendous discipline to stay the course of the original trading plan. It could be said that not every optimist is a sucker, but most suckers seem to be optimists. The optimist always thinks the market will move up in the long run. New institutional traders have a hard time believing the NASDAQ could implode day after day. Optimism is not restricted to the general public alone.

Beware of brokerage reports since the general public only buys stock and they want to be told to buy something to feed their greed. This is another reason you need to be mentally balanced to trade from the long or short side of a market. It keeps you objective.

One big mistake is trying to force the market to give you a fixed return. For example, I heard a trader say, "If the stock is only good for nine points, maybe I'd better buy something else or trade futures? I must have $x gain by the end of the month to pay for a tuition bill coming due." Whenever you *must* have a certain return, you are assured of having no return.

Another mistake is changing your trading style after a win. If a trader begins conservatively using a portion of his or her margin capability, nine out of ten traders will toss their caution to the wind when they have a profit. Any gains are often thought of as using someone else's money or the "house's money." Then when the account is margined to the maximum they discover they are forced on a small swing against them, only to see the market take off without them in the correct direction. It is always your money. Restrain yourself from making a crapshoot bet with all your chips on the table. The element-of-ruin will guarantee your loss because you cannot hold the swings against you that will inevitably come.

Markets are like ice cream on a hot day. You buy three large scoops of rocky road and when your friend orders the same, the waiter informs your dinner companion that they have just run out. Suddenly you look upon your bowl of ice cream as if it has greater value. Your friend offers to pay you more for the bowl. You agree, because you can't resist a profit. Your friend then tells you that it is the best ice cream he has ever tasted and you begin to wish you had not sold it to him. You offer him more and when the ice cream is passed back to you, it has melted. It neither has value nor offers satisfaction that you own it again.

Perhaps the next weakness that traders must learn to face is their own "will to believe." They think to be true whatever they *hope* is true. People who only buy often pin their faith to poor stocks and expect these to advance because this is their hope and salvation. Do you have chart evidence a stock will rally, or have you done very little homework and really mean, "Oh, if only it *would* go up!"? Is your market view an opinion based on knowledge and work on the evidence in your charts, or is it an opinion rooted in hope to bolster your courage?

In a panic, the weak stocks are not the ones people and fund managers dump. They sell the best stocks to raise cash because these are the easiest to sell and the most liquid. These become the targets because most people have already spent the profits they have on paper. The new car or boat is about to be paid in full by the market, but suddenly the money disappears and the boat remains on credit. Even imaginary purchases become part of our fiber as we conduct our lives as if we have already purchased something out of our unrealized gains. These are all head games a good trader must learn to control to be successful. People often fall victim to the "will to believe" trap. It's important to be cold and calculating when dealing with the markets. That is how the markets will be treating you.

You'll discover that illogical behavior is often the right course of action. Where market logic is concerned, the wrong behavior in the opinion of the mass crowd is often exceptional judgment in hindsight. Odd, but you can prosper when most think your logic is illogical and your chances for success can be greatly enhanced by doing what seems by most to be wrong. Markets move in a direction that is damaging to the most people, so to do well you have to think outside of the crowd and have the courage to walk in a different direction. To follow obvious group thinking is fatal since the majority does not win with longevity. As an example, you may notice a stock dropping in price when good news has entered the market on the company. You may notice the reverse when a stock rallies on bad news. This is because stocks often move into the news event as the mass crowd anticipates the outcome. Then when the news is released the stock reverses to show the selling (or buying) pressure is tapped out. In declines, some think the worse is out for the issue and that is reason to buy. You will discover that there is never so much good news to be said about a stock as on the day it reaches its record-high price. Stage magicians recognize this trait of human nature. A magician throw balls into the air, one after another until finally the last ball that he throws mysteriously disappears—only, he didn't throw the last one at all. By making the throwing motion the crowd is conditioned to assume that what happened in the past will repeat. Economists extrapolate based on the repeating series preceding the forecast as well. As a result, because you have arrived at a logical conclusion, on the very day you decide to buy you find the stock goes down, not up as it did before. Technical indicators can warn you when a trend is at a risky entry point. Patience can be rewarded allowing better timing without getting caught up in the emotions of the crowd. Capitulation washouts at the end of a vicious decline are an opportunity for the cold, calculating trader who sees the crowd panic and toss their good stocks into the abyss, driving the market to a major price zone of support. If the next decline follows with lower volume, it is confirmation the selling pressure is tapped out. Again this illustrates how good traders are independent and often buck the crowd's opinion.

Psychologists know that nearly all members of the human race are influenced somewhat by the day of the week. We feel different on Mondays than we do on Wednesday or Saturday. This also affects market participation. People like to sell into holidays like the July Fourth holiday in order to bank profits so they can enjoy their break. Then people start to buy them back after the holidays because they feel good and the optimists roll back into the market. Use the crowd as a contrarian point of view. Have computers changed these old perils of wisdom? It has certainly become faster to trade in current markets, but the crowd is no wiser because human character has not changed.

If two stocks are trading at $50 and I was to forecast they would both go up to $60, how would you know which to favor? It is essential that you look at the trading range of the stock. If the stock at $50 once traded at $274, this is not a big deal. If the second stock trading $50 has never traded over $51, this is significant. Which would you favor? I'll take the stock that has an underlying stock sector that matches the profile. Then I'll calculate the win-to-loss ratio used in Chapter 10. All this will work only if my indicators give permission at a specific price zone. But monitoring the range a stock trades within is something often overlooked.

An old accounting of the 1929 Great Crash describes a fascinating story. A psychologist, Fred Kelly wrote in a letter that a friend told him to buy a stock in November of 1929. It was reported, "Any stock that can resist that downpour of selling must be extra good," he reasoned, "therefore, when the turn does come, in a day or so, it will be the first stock to swing sharply upward."

He was right about the stock being good, but when a counter-trend bounce finally did occur, this stock went down because people sold anything to raise cash for buying bigger bargains. Here's a little more history about the media in 1929 being dead wrong. On a Sunday following the famous Tuesday crash of 1929, newspapers carried front-page headlines about the mood of buying orders that would swamp the market after the weekend. They were convinced so many bargain hunters would step forward it would swamp the order clerks. But Monday came and prices fell all day because the smart money wanted to use this sentiment hyped by the newspapers to raise any cash they could. Fred Kelly uses this contrarian tactic to illustrate a human trait he recognized, but still failed to heed, since he bought on his friend's advice and lost.

In his letter, Mr. Kelly reported:

…before the Big Crash of October 1929 the public had ample warning that the big fellows were selling and the little fellows buying. Week after week, the published report of the Federal Reserve Banks indicated that brokers' loans to the public were going up, even though average stock prices were declining. In other words, the growth in loans could not be explained by greater value of stocks. The figures could only show the number of margin accounts–stocks held by brokers for customers, with loans against them–were increasing, while people able to own their stock outright were selling.

This is a fascinating bit of historical record since today we have a specific data series called the *Commitment of Traders* to measure this exact sentiment. In this case the smart money was viewed as the large speculator not using margin. Today we measure the institutional activity against the small speculative trader, all in an effort to track the "smart money" and fade, or trade against a general public with a long history of being wrong. In Mr. Kelly's letter he made a fatal error and assumed a bottom. That is the same error many NASDAQ traders made from 2000 to 2003. Stocks making new lows can make even deeper declines.

Mr. Kelly further reported:

One of the reasons for the stupendous size of the selling panic [in October 1929] was probably this: When the first warning break came, early in October, the public, instead of selling, mistook the slightly lower prices for bargains and used every cash reserve to buy still more stocks. Naturally this added to the burden of protecting their holdings as prices fell. As prices went lower, the volume and speed of sales increased! But it is known the Morgans [J.P. Morgan] and the Rockefellers [John D.], bought at these extreme depressed prices. Papers reported John D. Rockefeller wanted to sell large blocks of Standard Oil of New Jersey in 1923, but then in 1929 was an aggressive buyer of Standard Oil at $49. In hindsight he bought his shares back from the public at considerable savings after using their money to boost his empire. But none of us wanted them when he bought, even if we had money left, because we reasoned: Stocks are in a violent downward trend. Therefore, they'll still go lower tomorrow! Whatever it is will always continue. We always seem to look behind us when we should be looking forward.

His account of October and November 1929 is hard to separate from today's markets in terms of mass sentiment. When the majority of public traders feel all is safe and nothing can happen, history will repeat with a slightly new twist. The mass psychology of crowds does not change, and that is why markets repeat cycles of fear and greed. To be a successful trader is to be a student of human nature and master of one's own human instincts. We use technical analysis to keep our human instincts in check.

Fred Kelly ended his letter of 1930 with much wisdom. He wrote:

"We gradually learn the tricks our nature uses to fool us. But unless we watch our step carefully, we don't learn soon enough—not until after our money is gone. The game is old—but the players are always new and will make the same mistakes."

Glossary

Advance-Decline Line (Indicator)   Calculates the difference between advancing issues and declining issues and plots the cumulative total of this value for the chart. The difference between advancing issues and declining issues is known as market breadth. For example, if a stock market index is rallying but there are more issues declining than advancing, then the rally is narrow and much of the stock market is not participating.

Ask (See also **Bid**)   The price at which a security, futures, or other financial instrument is offered for sale. Generally, the lowest round unit price at which a dealer will sell. Also, the per-share price at which a mutual fund share is offered to the public.

Ask Size (See also **Bid Size**)   The number of trading units a dealer is prepared to sell for a symbol.

Average (Indicator)   The average or moving average calculates the standard arithmetic mean of prices or values over a range of bars. It may also be called a moving average, since the values are recalculated for every bar. There are three types of averages used: simple, weighted, and exponential.

Bad Price Tick   A bad price tick means that an invalid price is broadcast by your quote vendor or the exchange. A bad price tick will appear as an unusual spike up or down on your charts. For example, if a symbol was trading at $45.78 and a tick was received as $89.45, followed by another tick at or near $45.78, you could assume the $89.45 value was a bad price tick.

Bar Charts   Bar charts can be time-based, tick-based, or volume-based. When using time-based data (intraday, daily, weekly, or monthly), each bar on the chart illustrates the open, high, low, and closing prices for the time increment represented by the bar.

> **Bar Types** *Candlestick Bar:* Uses the Japanese Candlestick charting style, which has the same components as the OHLC Bar but is displayed and interpreted differently. A "hollow" candlestick represents a rising market and a "filled" candlestick represents a declining market.
>
> *HLC Bar:* Displays the high, low, and close for each bar.
>
> *Line on Close:* Connects the close for each bar to the close of the preceding bar creating a line graph of closing prices only. In a chart with a 1-tick data interval, this bar style results in a chart where a solid line connects the price of all transactions.
>
> *OHLC Bar:* Displays the open, high, low, and close prices for each bar (this is the most common default option for vendors to use). In a chart with a daily data interval, this bar shows the open, high, low, and close for that day's session. The open is a small tick mark to the left of the bar. The close is on the right side of the bar. In a chart with a 1-tick data interval, the open, high, low, and close are the same because there is just one transaction. This results in a chart where a solid line connects the price of all transactions.

Bearish   Describes a market experiencing a period of falling prices. Bearish can also refer to a general expectation of declining prices.

Bear Market   A bear market is characterized by a prolonged period of declining prices.

Bearish Divergence   A move in the price of an asset not confirmed by a comparable move in the applied technical indicator. A bearish divergence exists when a market reaches a new high without the indicator reaching a corresponding new high.

Bearish Key Reversal   A bar pattern consisting of a bar whose high is greater than the previous bar's high, but ultimately closes lower than the previous bar's close.

Bearish Position   A bearish position is a market position benefiting from a decrease in price of a financial instrument.

Bid (See also **Ask**)   The highest price a prospective buyer is prepared to pay at a particular time for a trading unit of a given symbol.

Bid Size (See also **Ask Size**)   The number of trading units a prospective buyer is prepared to purchase for a symbol.

Bottom   The lowest price of a market during a specified period of time (that is, day, season, year, cycle, and so on).

Breakout   A breakout occurs when a market moves out of its trend channel. A market penetrating through its support or resistance level is said to have "broken out" of its current trend. Markets tend to continue to move in the same direction as the breakout.

Bull Market   A market characterized by a prolonged period of rising prices usually accompanied by high trading volume.

Bullish Divergence   A move in the price of an asset not confirmed by a comparable move in the applied technical indicator. A bullish divergence occurs when market prices reach a new low without the indicator reaching a corresponding new low.

Bullish Key Reversal   A bar whose low is lower than the previous bar's low, but ultimately closes higher than the previous bar's close.

Bullish Position   A market position benefiting from an increase in price of a financial instrument.

Buy Limit Order A buy order that won't be executed until the price falls to a specified amount.

Buy Stop Order A buy order only executed if and when the market reaches a specified price.

Buy-to-Cover A trading order used to cover a short position.

Chicago Board Of Trade (CBOT) The CBOT is a futures exchange. Its session times and price increments are defined on a per-market basis.

Chicago Mercantile Exchange (CME)(GLOBEX) The CME allows the trading of futures contracts outside the normal day session using the GLOBEX platform. Orders can be placed between 5:00 p.m. Sunday night and 8:00 p.m. Friday night Eastern Time. Orders are not queued; any order placed outside the hours of operation will be rejected.

Close The closing price of the current day, exclusive of Form T trades (a trade executed outside of the normal trade reporting day).

Close Tick The price of the final transaction during the period of time represented by the bar.

Correlation A statistics function that calculates the correlation coefficient between an independent and dependent data series.

Correlation Coefficient A number between −1 and 1, which measures the degree to which two variables are related linearly. If there is a perfect linear relationship with positive slope between the two variables, there is a correlation coefficient of 1; if there is a positive correlation, whenever one variable has a high (low) value, the other does also. If there is a perfect linear relationship with negative slope between the two variables, there is a correlation coefficient of −1; if there is a negative correlation, whenever one variable has a high (low) value, the other has a low (high) value. A correlation coefficient of 0 means that there is no linear relationship between the variables.

Cycles (Time) A time cycle is an analytic drawing tool used to identify cyclical price activity–repeating high and low price patterns. Cycle analysis is based on the premise that a market's price activity behaves in patterns. Therefore, future price activity can be predicted by identifying historical price patterns. It can be difficult to identify a cycle; identification may require analyzing years of data. Once you identify a repeating price pattern, the time cycle can assist you in determining the time intervals between those patterns.

Identifying cycles can provide insight as to how long a particular trend or pattern will continue. Analysts following cycles believe when a cycle bottoms (reaches its trough), an up trend will follow until the cycle tops out (reaches its crest). Once the crest is reached, a down trend continues until the cycle reaches its trough and the cycle begins again.

Daily Bars   Daily bars plot the price of a symbol on a daily basis. Each bar represents one day of trading.

Data Analysis   The process of studying market price movement, price history, and supply and demand to determine in what direction a market will move. Analysis of data involves creating charts and applying various analysis techniques to determine price patterns and market signals. These patterns and signals help indicate specific market direction, which, in turn, assist in understanding the market.

Data Analysis Terminology   (See Gaps, Overbought/Oversold, Trending Market, Sideways Market, Support and Resistance, and Volatile Market)

Data Interval   A data interval represents the amount of price action within a bar (from the open to the close) and is expressed either in terms of time (1 minute, 30 minute, daily, etc.) or trading activity (tick count or volume). For example, in a daily chart each bar interval represents the price action of one day--the bar opens in the morning with the beginning of the trading session and closes at the end of the trading session in the afternoon, and so on for each bar.

Depth   The number of market makers offering a specific bid and specific ask price. The number of market makers behind the bid is listed first, separated from the number of market makers behind the ask by an asterisk (*). For example, 9 * 4 indicates that there are 9 market makers behind a specific bid and 4 market makers behind a specific ask.

Divergence (See also Bearish Divergence and Bullish Divergence)   A move in the price of an asset not confirmed by a comparable move in the applied technical indicator. For example, a bullish divergence exists when a market reaches a new low without the indicator reaching a corresponding new low. Conversely, a bearish divergence exists when a market reaches a new high without the indicator reaching a corresponding new high.

Downtick (See also **Uptick**)   A downtick is a tick that is lower than the previous tick (or the same as the previous tick).

FOREX (Foreign Exchange Currency)   The symbology for FOREX symbols is a six-character symbol consisting of two three-character pairs. The first three-character pair is the base currency and the second three-character pair is the counter currency. The symbol trades in lots, where each lot consists of 100,000 units of the base currency. For example, EURUSD is the symbol for trading Euros that are calculated in US dollars.

Fundamental Analysis   Fundamental analysis, primarily used to analyze stocks, is the study of financial data such as corporate earnings and financial statements as well as the economic factors that influence supply and demand to forecast price movement.

Gap or Gaps   An occurrence in a bar chart where the low is above the high of the previous day, or the high is below the previous day's low. Either of these situations will cause a gap between the bars that can be seen when the market is charted.

Many factors can cause prices to move significantly enough to cause price gaps. For example, earnings reports or good economic news within a particular industry can lead to gaps.

Head and Shoulders Pattern   Named for the chart pattern resembling a head with two shoulders. The first shoulder is created as prices make higher highs and higher lows. As this trend loses momentum, prices retrace to the neckline and then begin to trend up farther than the first shoulder creating the head. Prices then retrace to the neckline and then the first shoulder pattern is repeated to create the second shoulder.

Intra-day Bars   Intraday bars plot the price of a symbol over a specified number of minutes. For example, you can plot 1-minute bars, 5-minute bars, 10-minute bars, and so on. A new intra-day bar is built every x-minutes (where x is the number of minutes specified).

Long-term Versus Short-term Charts   The data interval and time frame for a chart are determining factors as to whether you are able to accurately study data for short-term or long-term market activity. Short-term is usually considered a month or less. Creating charts to analyze short-term price activity can help you identify minor adjustments in market direction or a short correction in price movement. Tick, intraday, and daily data intervals are primarily used for short-term data analysis.

Long-term data analysis involves a time frame anywhere from one week to several years. Long-term charts are the best way to accurately identify strong bullish and bearish markets. Charts with a daily data interval can be used for long-term analysis. However, weekly and monthly charts are generally used because they provide the best overall picture of price and market activity.

Long-term Trend   A long-term trend is a movement in the market sustained over a relatively long period of time.

Low Tick   The lowest price for any transaction during the period of time represented by the bar.

Moving Average Convergence Divergence (MACD) (Indicator)   The MACD calculates 2 exponential moving averages of the lengths specified by the inputs FastLength and SlowLength. The difference between these 2 averages is then plotted as the MACD. This value is also averaged for the number of bars specified by the input MACDLength and then plotted as the MACDAvg. Finally, the difference between the MACD and the MACD average is calculated and plotted as the MACDDiff. As a trend-following indicator, the MACD may be interpreted similarly to other moving averages. When the MACD crosses above the MACD Average, it may be the beginning of an up trend. Conversely, when the MACD crosses below the MACD Average, it may be the beginning of a down trend. As an oscillator, the MACD can indicate overbought and oversold conditions.

Margin Debit   The amount that you are borrowing when trading on a margin account. For example, if you deposit $50,000 to trade stocks in your margin account, you will have $100,000 in buying power. If you buy $60,000 in securities, you are borrowing $10,000 over your actual deposit, so your margin debt is $10,000.

Market Maker   A member firm of the National Association of Securities Dealers (NASD). NASD relies on market makers to provide liquidity in over-the-counter

(OTC) securities. A market maker is the equivalent of a specialist for the NYSE or ASE. Each market maker is required to be both a buyer and a seller of the securities that they represent. Their goal is to combine their efforts in each stock to collectively support a two-sided market.

Market Order (See **Order Types**)   An order to buy at whatever the best price is at the time the order reaches the trading floor.

Moving Average   An asset's average calculated over a specified period of time. For example, a 30-bar moving average includes the last 30 bars of an asset's value in its calculation. The next day, the moving average replaces the earliest bar (which is now the thirty-first day) with the most recent bar to calculate the current bar's moving average. Moving averages are often used to obtain a smoothed value of an asset.

Neutral   Used to describe a non-trending or sideways market. Neutral markets do not move significantly away from established high and low prices.

New High   Occurs when the current high exceeds the previous highest high for a defined period of time (that is, the current move, specified number of trailing bars, entire data series, and so on).

New Low   A new low occurs when the current low is less than the previous lowest low for a defined period of time (that is, the current move, specified number of trailing bars, entire data series, and so on).

Open Position   Occurs when you have entered into either a long or short trade and have not yet exited. After you establish a long position, you have an open long position until you liquidate all long shares or contracts. Likewise, you have an open short position until you close out the position.

Optimization   The process of testing a range of values used for inputs with the purpose of fine-tuning a trading strategy. Optimization is used to enhance a trading idea; it cannot be used to develop one.

Order Durations   The length of time that your order will remain valid in the market. The durations available may vary depending on the selected order route. Some vendors do not offer all of the possible durations.

If you want to enter a position but want to wait for a breakout (or rally) and subsequent retracement before entering the market, you can use a stop limit

Duration	Description	Supporting Routes
At-The-Market	Fill immediately at the best possible price	
Day	Valid until the end of the extended trading session.	
FOK	(Fill or Kill) FOK orders are filled in their entirety or canceled. Partial fills are not accepted when using this order duration.	NSDQ
GTC	(Good till Canceled)	
GTD	(Good till Date)	
IOC	(Immediate or Cancel) IOC orders are filled immediately or canceled. Partial fills are accepted when using this order duration.	ARCA BTRD NSDQ

order. For example, if the market is trading at 54, you can place a Buy Stop Limit order at 55 for 55.05. This means that when the price reaches 55, a limit order is set for 55.05, so your buy order can be executed only at a price of 55.05 or below.

Note: The Stop price must be better than the current market price at the time the order is sent in and the Limit price must be at or better the stop price. In addition, the limit part of the order only becomes visible to the market after the stop price has been reached, although there is no guarantee that the limit price will be met.

Order Types

Order Type	Description
buy limit order	A buy order that won't be executed until the price falls to a specified amount.
buy stop order	A buy order only executed if and when the market reaches a specified price.
limit order	An order executed only once the price reaches a specific level. When you are in a short position and request a limit order, it will be executed only if the price falls to the specified level.
limit order to sell	A sell order that won't be executed unless the price reaches a specific level that you indicate.
market order	An order to buy at whatever the best price is at the time the order reaches the trading floor.
sell stop order	A sell order executed only if and when the market falls to a specific price that you indicate.
stop limit order	A stop limit order combines the features of a stop order and a limit order. After the stop price is reached, the stop server sends a limit order; the order is then executed at the specified limit price or better, market conditions permitting.
stop loss order	In the case of a long position, a sell order to close if the price falls to a specific amount that you set. In the case of a short position, a buy order to close if the price rises to a specific amount that you set.

Overbought/Oversold   Both of these market conditions occur when a market's price has reached an extreme level. An overbought market is one where the price has risen too far and may need to pause at its current price level, or even possibly fall. An oversold market is when a market has fallen in price too far and will most likely turn upward, at least in the short term. A general guideline for determining overbought and oversold markets is that when a market doubles in price, it is usually overbought, and when a market's price drops in half, the market is oversold.

Profit/Loss (P/L)   The unrealized profit or loss on the position held.

Price   The actual value of a financial instrument.

Pyramiding   Technically, pyramiding involves using unrealized profits from one securities or commodities position as collateral to buy further positions with funds borrowed from a broker.

Range   The highest and lowest prices, or the difference between them, for a bar or any other given interval.

Rebound   A period of regained strength in a market following a decline.

Resistance (See also **Support and Resistence**)   Resistance refers to the peaks that represent a prior high or series of highs identified on a chart. A resistance level lies over the market and indicates a period where selling pressure overcomes buying pressure that turns the price downward. In other words, resistance indicates a level above which the price "resists" rising. If a market's price breaks above a prior established resistance level, it may indicate that a price's move upward is continuing or beginning. If, however, the prices are not moving past the resistance level, that is, closing below the resistance, this could indicate a reversal in price direction, or an indication of a sideways market not moving up or down significantly.

Retracement   Occurs when a market corrects itself after it trends up or down significantly. For example, if a market moves from 10 to 40 followed by a move down to 30, the market is said to have retraced from 40 to 30.

Reversal   A change in the price direction of a market. For example, if Microsoft steadily climbs from 70 to 90, a reversal is said to take place if the price begins a sustained fall back toward 70.

Reversal and Continuation Patterns   Many chart patterns are indicative of trend direction, and have been used for many years by chart analysts. Most patterns will indicate either a change, or reversal, in trend, or the continuation of the current trend. In fact, the support and resistance level concept is basic in recognizing chart patterns. The most common trend reversal patterns are double and triple tops and bottoms, and head and shoulders. The popular continuation pattern is the triangle. All of these patterns only require the ability to spot peaks and troughs on a chart.

Double and Triple Tops and Bottoms: In an up trend, a double top is a price chart with two prominent peaks at around the same high. The triple top is three prominent peaks, meaning that the sideways movement continued longer. If the price closes higher than the prior peaks, the up trend will probably be resumed. However, if the price declines below its prior peak and begins to weaken, a trend reversal may be beginning.

A double bottom is a mirror of the double top, as well as for the triple top. If a chart shows two or three prominent lows at around the same price, and the price closes above the prior low, a new up trend may be indicated.

Head and Shoulders: This pattern is similar to the triple bottom in that it uses three prominent lows. The difference in the head and shoulders pattern is the one prominent low in the middle with two slightly higher lows on either side resembling someone standing on their head. This is a bottoming pattern. When a trend line is drawn above the two peaks on either side of the prominent low, and a price breaks through that line, a new up trend may be beginning. The top pattern is exactly the opposite and is sometimes referred to as an inverse head and shoulders.

Triangle: This pattern usually indicates a market that has risen or fallen too far or too fast and needs to consolidate (or pull back into a more sideways direction). Once the market consolidation is complete, the market usually resumes its prior trend. Because of this, the triangle is referred to as bullish in an up trend and bearish in a down trend.

The triangle can be identified by sideways price activity where the price action begins to narrow. If trend lines were drawn at the peaks and troughs, they would appear to converge. An ascending triangle, considered to be bullish, has a flat trend line at the high end of the price range, while the line along the bottom is rising. The descending triangle, considered to be bearish, has a flat trend line at the bottom with a falling line at the high end of the price range.

Short Describes a market position benefiting from a price decrease. You are "going short" when you open a position to sell a security, commodity, or some other financial market. You are most likely bearish toward that financial instrument because you are selling in anticipation of a decrease in price. When you "go short," you are actually borrowing shares or contracts from a brokerage firm in order to sell them. If the market maintains its bearish trend, you can buy those shares at a lower cost at a later time to fulfill your loan commitment while simultaneously making a profit. To open a short position, you must establish a margin account with your brokerage house.

Short-term Trend   A short-term trend, otherwise known as a near-term trend, describes a market's movement sustained over a relatively short period of time.

Sideways Market   A sideways market moves with very little variation between the high and low price and is referred to as trendless. It can also be referred to as a market that is trading within a range. Identifying a sideways market is important.

Many analysts advise against buying or selling in this type of market and prefer to monitor the market until some sort of direction can be identified. Data analysis can help you identify a sideways market and identify when it is beginning to make a significant move either up or down (referred to as a "breakout").

Slippage   The difference in price between when you place an order and when the order is executed.

Spread   The difference between the best bid and the best ask for a specific symbol. For example, if the best bid is 501/4 and the best ask is 501/2, the spread is 1/4.

Stall   A resting point or plateau in a market. For example, a significant up trend might be followed by a resting period where the market stalls before continuing the current trend or possibly reversing direction.

Standard Deviation   Standard deviation is a statistical concept that illustrates how a specific set of prices is divided or spread around an average value. The concept is that 68 percent of data values differ from the middle average value by less than one standard deviation, and that 95 percent of data values differ from the middle average by less than two standard deviations.

Support (See also **Support and Resistance**)   Support refers to the troughs and indicates a prior low, or series of lows, identified on a chart. Support levels always lie under the market and indicate a period where buying interest is strong enough to overcome selling pressure that turns the price up. In other words, support illustrates a level that "supports" the price from falling below. Price movement below a defined support level may warn that a down trend is occurring or continuing. Price movement bouncing up from the support level may indicate that a down trend is ending, or that prices have gone as far down as they are going to, at least for a period of time. Many analysts believe when a market is falling toward its support level it is "testing its support," meaning that it could rebound after it hits the support level. If the market penetrates through the support level, it is considered extremely bearish.

Support and Resistance These two terms help to describe highs (peaks) and lows (troughs) that can be seen when charting a specific market. The price movement of that market in relationship to these peaks and troughs can help you determine whether that market will stay on course, reverse its course, or not move at all.

Technical Analysis The study of market price activity. Technical analysts view any factor influencing a market to be reflected in the price of that market. By monitoring the movement of the price data, supply and demand market trends can be determined.

Technical analysis can be defined as an approach to market forecasting that involves studying current and historical market price, volume, and in the case of futures, open interest. John Murphy, author of several well-known books on technical analysis, defines technical analysis as "the study of market action, primarily through the use of charts, for the purpose of forecasting future price trends." Some analysts believe technical analysis also involves the study of human behavior as it relates to market trends and the laws of probability. Technical analysts believe that market history repeats itself, and that the historical trends and patterns that illustrate bearish and bullish markets will be seen again in the future.

Testing Testing a strategy is a two-step process. First, test your trading rules on historical data (also called backtesting) to examine the results that are generated. Once they perform sufficiently to your requirements, you can apply the rules in a computer and automate them to see how they perform in real time. Complete strategy testing involves both historical and real-time evaluation.

Tick Bars Tick bars plot the price of each transaction. Tick bars differ from time-based bars because tick bars plot prices based on a transaction-by-transaction basis while time-based bars plot prices during a specified time period. A transaction can represent 100 shares, 200 shares, 1,000 shares, and so on. When plotting tick bars, price and number of ticks are the only factors used, as time and volume are not considered.

For example, you can create a 5-tick chart, where one bar is comprised of the open, high, low, and closing ticks for each set of 5 ticks. The length of time in that 5-tick bar could be a few seconds, a minute, an hour, or even a day.

In a 1-tick chart, there is no reason to report the open, high, low, and closing prices because the exact trade price is plotted. In a 1-tick bar chart, the open, high, low, and closing price are the same. Therefore, when creating a chart consisting of 1-tick bars, the price data is not really displayed as a bar but rather a series of connected ticks.

When you create a tick-based chart where each bar contains a certain number of ticks, each bar contains the range of open, high, low, and closing prices for a specified number of ticks (for example, 10 ticks, 100 ticks, 1000 ticks, and so on). When you change the data interval to build bars based on multiple ticks-per-bar, the bars look exactly like time-based bars in that they plot the open, high, low, and closing prices for the specified number of transactions.

Top   Refers to the highest price of an asset during a specified period of time (that is, day, season, year, cycle, and so on). A top is often viewed as a resistance level for market prices.

Trend   A trend represents the direction in which a market is going. A market price will move in a zig-zag fashion creating peaks and troughs. The trend or direction of a market price will be determined by the direction of those peaks and troughs.

In general, the longer a trend has been moving in that trending direction, the more significant that trend is. The direction of a trend will be either up, down, or sideways. This corresponds to bullish, bearish, and sideways markets. Trends can also be categorized as major, intermediate, and near-term; however there are an infinite number of ways in which trends interact with each other on a single chart.

Trend Lines   Trends can be illustrated using trend lines. When applying trend lines, you will be able to view various chart patterns that can help you identify and predict the strength of a trend and whether a trend reversal may occur.

Trend lines are used to determine the slope of a trend and to help identify or indicate when a trend is changing. Generally, trend lines are drawn to identify and follow up trends and down trends (sideways trend lines can also be drawn, however, they would be more indicative of a support or a resistance level).

An up trend line is drawn under rising lows (or troughs), and a down trend line is drawn above declining highs (or peaks). A trend line should include all price activity and touch troughs or peaks two to three times. Obviously, the more times prices bounce off of the trend line to test its validity, the more significant the trend line becomes.

Most analysts draw several trend lines on their charts measuring and identifying near-term, intermediate and long-term trends. They will also add or change existing trend lines when the original trend line is either no longer applicable or incorrect.

Trending Market A trending market is characterized by sustained increases or decreases in price movement, and can be bullish or bearish. There may be small fluctuations (small and short-lived corrections) in price along the way, but the overall character is trending. A bullish trending market is a market in which data indicates an upswing, or rise, in price. Most investors recommend buying into a bullish market. It is optimal to buy at the beginning of the market upswing (or up trend).

Conversely, a bearish trending market is a market in which data indicates a downswing, or drop in price. Most investors recommend going short in a bearish market, with the optimum timing being at the beginning of the drop. The closer to the beginning of the down trend you go short, the better your potential for making money.

The data interval you use can significantly impact the character of the market. For example, the same chart that exhibits trending conditions in a daily chart can exhibit sideways conditions in a monthly chart. You should evaluate the chart using the data interval you plan to trade.

Triangle Pattern A triangle pattern is identified by sideways price activity where the price action begins to narrow. If trend lines were drawn at the peaks and troughs, they would appear to converge. An ascending triangle has a flat trend line at the high end of the price range while the line along the bottom is rising. The descending triangle has a flat trend line at the bottom with a falling line at the high end of the price range.

True High The higher of the current bar's high and the previous bar's close. True high accounts for gaps between bars when calculating range.

True Low The lesser of the current bar's low and the previous bar's close. True low accounts for gaps between bars when calculating range.

True Range The highest true high and lowest true low prices, or the difference between them, for a bar or any other given interval. True range accounts for gaps between bars when calculating range.

Upticks (See also **Downtick**) An uptick is a tick that is higher than the previous tick (or the same as the previous tick). Adding upticks and downticks together provides the total number of ticks.

Volatile Market Characterized by significant movement, either up or down, in price. Market that trend day after day in the same direction have low volatility.

Volume Bars   Volume bars plot bars based on a specified trade volume. For example, you can plot bars every time a certain number of shares are sold; for example, when 100, 200, or 1,000 shares are sold. A new volume bar is built every x-number of shares sold (where x is the volume you specify).

Volume bars record the open, high, low, and closing prices for a specified volume of shares traded. Volume-based bar charts are helpful for traders interested in analyzing trading volume.

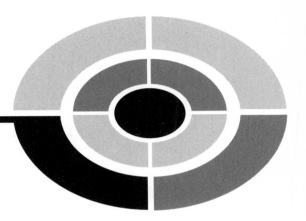

Answers to Quiz Questions

Chapter One	Chapter Two	Chapter Three
1. c.	1. c.	1. b.
2. d.	2. a.	2. a.
3. b.	3. b.	3. e.
4. e.	4. c.	4. e.
5. d.	5. c.	5. d.
6. d.	6. d.	6. e.
7. e.	7. c.	7. e.
8. d.	8. b.	8. d.
9. d.	9. e.	9. a.
10. d.	10. d.	10. e.

Chapter Four

1. c.
2. a.
3. d.
4. b.
5. c.
6. a.
7. b.
8. d.
9. c.
10. b.

Chapter Five

1. b.
2. c.
3. a.
4. d.
5. b.
6. a.
7. d.
8. c.
9. a.
10. b.

Chapter Six

All answers are True.

Chapter Seven

1. b.
2. a.
3. d.
4. b.
5. c.
6. e.
7. a.
8. b.
9. c.
10. b.

Chapter Eight

1–8 are True.
9. e.
10. e.

Chapter Nine

1. c.
2. b.
3. d.
4. e.
5. c.
6. a.
7. b.
8. c.
9. d.
10. e.

INDEX

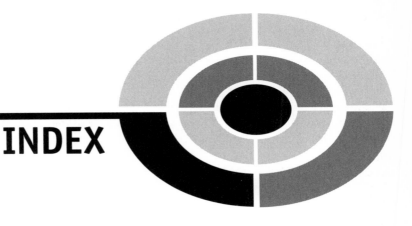

Index

Index

U

V

W

Y

Z

About the Author

Connie Brown, CMT (Chartered Market Technician), founded Aerodynamic Investments Inc. (www.aeroinvest.com) after working more than 15 years as an institutional trader in New York City. She continues to trade actively from her equestrian estate in South Carolina and advises numerous financial institutions and banks around the world through the Internet. She now has over 70 students who have moved on to manage assets or work for major institutions. Seminars and lectures are viewed as an important part of contributing to the development of technical analysis.

Ms. Brown's second book, *Technical Analysis for the Trading Professional,* was selected by the Market Technicians Association as required reading to prepare for CMTIII, the third and final examination that awards professionals the industry's Chartered Market Technician accreditation. She is also a member of the American Association of Professional Technical Analysts. Ms. Brown has written six books.